Building for God's glory

Building for God's glory

Haggai and Zechariah
simply explained

by

Michael Bentley

 EVANGELICAL PRESS

EVANGELICAL PRESS
Faverdale North Industrial Estate, Darlington, DL3 0PH, England

Evangelical Press USA
P. O. Box 84, Auburn, MA 01501, USA

e-mail: sales@evangelical-press.org

web: www.evangelical-press.org

First published 1989
Second impression 1999

British Library Cataloguing in Publication Data:

Bentley, Michael
Building for God's glory: Haggai and Zechariah simply explained
1. Bible. O.T. Haggai. Critical studies.
2. Bible. O.T. Zechariah. Critical studies
I. Title. II. Series
224'.9706

ISBN 0 85234-259-4

Typeset by Outset Graphics, Hartlepool
Printed and bound in Great Britain by Cox & Wyman Ltd., Reading

In loving memory of
SIMON PHILIP BENTLEY
who was suddenly called to be
with his Lord on 22 November 1987,
aged eighteen years and twenty-three days.

Contents

Preface

'What's your book going to be about?' asked my blind piano tuner as I was driving him to his next appointment. 'It's a commentary on Haggai and Zechariah', I replied. 'That's interesting,' he said, with a puzzled tone in his voice. 'Who were they?' Immediately it flashed through my mind that my friend was probably imagining that I was writing a book about some long-forgotten warlike clans from Scotland.

When I started to preach through Haggai's prophecy, many of our congregation were just as ignorant of the Old Testament prophets as my companion on that day. But as we examined these books we learned of God's desire that his temple, the church of Jesus Christ, should be rebuilt and reinvigorated in these days.

This is not a technical commentary and I have tried to avoid controversial matters which do not encourage spiritual growth. As over half of our congregation are new to church services, and therefore have not been brought up to sit through long sermons, my preaching has to be simple, clear and with the assumption that the people have no previous background knowledge of the Bible and its teaching. It is my hope that this book meets the same criteria and will encourage us all to 'search the Scriptures' and apply their teachings to our own lives.

I have been helped by so many people in the preparation of this book that it is impossible to mention them all but my special thanks go to the Rev. J. D. Legg for all his help and encouragement. Without the patient, efficient and speedy typing of Mrs Betty Clarkson (my mother-in-law and faithful church labourer) the task would have been infinitely more difficult. I am most grateful for all her hard work and her deciphering of my handwriting.

Michael Bentley
Bracknell
March 1989

Haggai

1.
Before the rebuilding started

When we come to study Haggai the first problem we face is to find it in our Bibles. It is not one of those books to which we turn regularly, nor is it a large book and therefore easy to find. Apart from Obadiah, it is the smallest book in the Old Testament. It comprises only two chapters, which total a mere thirty-eight verses. While it borrows ideas from Deuteronomy (compare Haggai 1:6 with Deuteronomy 28:38-40 and 2:17 with Deuteronomy 28:22) only one verse (2:6) is quoted in the New Testament (Hebrews 12:26).

Haggai himself is only mentioned in one other biblical book, the book of Ezra. In Ezra 5:1 and 6:14 we read about the work of Haggai in encouraging the Jews to rebuild the temple of the Lord, but these references do not throw any extra light on him and they refer to the same period of time as that covered in his prophecy.

No one ever argues about the date of the book. Each of the four brief prophecies it contains is clearly dated. They took place during the second year of the reign of King Darius Hystaspes of Babylon, which corresponds to the year 520 B.C.

The prophet

No mention is made of Haggai's parents or any of his ancestors. He came on to the scene without any prior announcement, gave his brief messages from God and then, less than four months later, disappeared from off the pages of history as suddenly as he came.

What can we learn about this man? Perhaps he came from
a lowly family. This may explain why his father is not mentioned. While Jewish tradition says he was a young priest
when he returned from the Babylonian exile, we have nothing
in Scripture to substantiate or deny this. He could equally
have been a very old man who had seen, with his own eyes,
the glories of Solomon's temple before it had been destroyed
by Nebuchadnezzar some sixty-six years earlier. Some scholars believe this to be the case because of his reference in chapter 2:3 to the former glory of the temple. Either way it matters
little. God has not told us whether he was young or old, tall or
short, fat or thin. If they were important to our understanding
of God's Word or stimulating to our spiritual life then God
would have made these things crystal clear. Let us always be
content with God's Word as it stands and not spend our time
in idle speculation like the philosophers of Paul's day on the
Areopagus (Acts 17:21).

Although we know nothing about Haggai's family, we can
perhaps gain a clue about him from his name. Names were
often given to describe the baby, commemorate some event
or express a wish for the child's future. Many scholars believe
that the name 'Haggai' is derived from *Hag*, which means
'festival' (see Genesis 46:16; Numbers 26:15; 2 Samuel 3:4;
1 Chronicles 6:30 for other names derived from the same
root). It seems likely that he was born on a feast day and
therefore named 'my feast'. Joyce Baldwin suggests that
'Haggai' may have been a nickname[1] and Robert Hawker
says that the name comes from the Hebrew word, *'chagag'*,
'to dance,' meaning a season of joy.[2]

What we do know is that he was one of a dying breed. There
had been many 'spoken' and 'written' prophets in Israel and
Judah in the preceding centuries but by the time of Haggai the
number of those who held the office of prophet was
diminishing.[3]

Haggai was a contemporary of Zechariah (compare Haggai
1:1 with Zechariah 1:1). They both urged the leaders of the
Jews, Zerubbabel and Joshua, as well as the people, to
resume the work of rebuilding the temple. Together with
Malachi (and possibly Joel) they comprise what are called
'the Post-Exilic Prophets'. Because they were concerned
about rebuilding the temple and restoring the worship of

God's house, they are often called by a name which is currently in vogue, 'the Restorationists'.

Apart from the central message to awake out of lethargy and build the Lord's house, Zechariah and Haggai are of great value as sources of information regarding a sparsely documented period of history, the years between the return to Palestine and the work of Ezra and Nehemiah.[4]

Haggai's prophetic life may have been brief but it was certainly successful. Together with Zechariah he was one of the few prophets who lived to see the fulfilment of his words. Haggai's message is expressly stated to have greatly helped the work forward (Ezra 5:1).[5]

The prophecy of Haggai is part of God's Word. It has a vital bearing on Christian life today and it repays careful and prayerful study. Do not just dip into it to meditate on a few favourite verses, but spend a little time examining what God is saying to you and God's people through this small but challenging prophecy.

Some necessary history

T.V. Moore argues that 'Prophecy, in some form, must co-exist with all history, that God's will may be known and performed by man.'[6] Some of us were taught in Sunday School that 'History is his [God's] story.' When we examine the tone and contents of any Old Testament prophecy we realize that it is impossible to understand its general drift without considering what was happening in the world at that time.

First of all we need to go back in time a little way. In the year 722 B.C. the ten northern tribes (Israel or Ephraim) had been taken captive by the Assyrians. They were cruelly treated and never returned to their homeland. For the next 136 years the southern kingdom of Judah plodded on through a few good times (under Hezekiah and Josiah) and very many bad ones (under Manasseh, Jehoahaz, Jehoiakim and Jehoiachin).

Then in about the year 586 B.C. Jerusalem was invaded by Nebuchadnezzar, who took most of its inhabitants away captive to Babylon. Only the poorest people of the land were left behind to work the vineyards and fields (2 Kings 25:11-12). In

2 Kings 25 and Jeremiah 52 we read the horrifying details of the destruction of Jerusalem. Nebuchadnezzar 'set fire to the temple of the Lord, the royal palace and all the buildings of Jerusalem. Every important building he burned down... The Babylonians broke up the bronze pillars, the movable stands and the bronze Sea that were at the temple of the Lord and they carried the bronze to Babylon. They also took away the pots, shovels, wick trimmers, ladles and all the bronze articles used in the temple service' (2 Kings 25:9, 13-14).

For about fifty years the Jews remained in captivity. While some settled down to make a good living in their exile many longed to return to their homeland. Their lament is recorded in Psalm 137:

> 'By the rivers of Babylon, we sat down and wept
>   When we remembered Zion.
> There on the poplars
>   we hung our harps,
> for there our captors asked us for songs,
>   our tormentors demanded songs of joy;
>   they said, "Sing us one of the songs of Zion!"
>
> How can we sing the songs of the Lord
>   while in a foreign land?
> If I forget you, O Jerusalem,
>   may my right hand forget its skill.
> May my tongue cling to the roof of my mouth
>   if I do not remember you,
> if I do not consider Jerusalem
>   my highest joy.'

(Psalm 137:1-6).

Then God miraculously intervened. A Persian invader captured Babylon. Isaiah had foretold that this man, Cyrus, would be raised up. 'He is my shepherd and will accomplish all that I please; [said the Lord] he will say of Jerusalem, "Let it be rebuilt," and of the temple, "Let its foundations be laid"' (Isaiah 44:28). This foreign ruler was the means by which the Jews returned to their homeland.

It would be most helpful if you would now put down this book, turn to your Bible and read Ezra chapters 1 to 4. You may skip the names in chapter 2, but just notice how many of these people who returned to Judah were connected with the worship of God. There were priests, Levites, gatekeepers of the temple, singers and temple servants – a total of nearly 5,700 out of 42,360, a proportion of 1 in 7½.[7]

When you reach the end of Ezra 4 in verse 24 you will read, 'Thus the work on the house of God in Jerusalem came to a standstill until the second year of the reign of Darius king of Persia.' This brings us to 29 August 520 B.C.[8]

The temple at Jerusalem

For many years after the children of Israel had settled in the promised land the ark of the covenant rested in a mere tent. King David had long wanted to build a house for God's glory but God did not permit him to do so because he was stained with the blood of his enemies. However, he was allowed to collect materials, gather treasure and buy the site from Araunah (1 Chronicles 22:3-4,8; 2 Samuel 24:18-25). His son Solomon then spent seven years building this wonderful 'house of God's presence'. 1 Kings 6 – 7 and 2 Chronicles 3 – 4 give us details of this temple. It was a glorious building with much lavish golden decoration. In its centre was a perfect cube of twenty cubits. This was the Holy of Holies. It was in this most sacred place that the ark of the covenant stood.

During the exile in Babylon the Jews longed to be able to worship in this temple which was at Jerusalem (the only place where God had given instructions for a temple). How shattered they must have been when they heard that it had been completely destroyed! They must have felt that they were for ever cut off from God. But while they were in captivity Ezekiel, speaking the Word of God, declared, 'I will make a covenant of peace with them [i.e. the Jews in captivity]; it will be an everlasting covenant. I will establish them and increase their numbers, and I will put my sanctuary among them for ever. My dwelling-place will be with them; I will be their God, and they will be my people' (Ezekiel 37:26-27).

The fact that God had made a covenant with them made it imperative for the Jews to rebuild the Jerusalem temple as soon as they returned to their homeland. 'The Lord overruled

international events (Zech. 1:18-21) and stirred up
enthusiasm through Haggai and Zechariah. The completion
of the temple was to be the proof that Zechariah had been
[God's] instrument (Zech. 4:9) and therefore a sign that the
covenant had been renewed.'[9]

Zerubbabel's temple, which is what the prophecy of Haggai
is all about, stood for nearly 500 years. It was enlarged by
King Herod the Great in an effort to impress the Jews and
make his rule more acceptable to them; and then, before it
was barely finished, it was utterly destroyed by the Romans in
A.D. 70. Jesus had predicted that this would happen: 'The
days will come upon you when your enemies will build an
embankment against you and encircle you and hem you in on
every side. They will dash you to the ground, you and the children within your walls. They will not leave one stone on
another' (Luke 19:42-44).

Since A.D. 70 the temple site has been bereft of a building
dedicated to Jehovah; although many efforts, encouraged by
some fundamentalist groups, especially in the U.S.A., have
been made to make plans for the rebuilding of the temple
prior to the second coming of our Lord.

Why has the temple at Jerusalem never been rebuilt?
Firstly, since A.D. 691 a Muslim mosque, the Dome of the
Rock, has stood on the site of the temple. This prominent
edifice dominates the skyline of the Israeli capital and is
firmly protected as the third most holy spot in Islam. It was
said that from this place the prophet Muhammad ascended
into heaven. Today no religious Jew will set foot upon this site
for fear that he might tread upon the spot where the Holy of
Holies once stood.

The second reason why there is no temple now is far more
important: today we have no need of an earthly temple building. Do you recall what happened when Jesus died on the
cross? The veil that separated the Holy of Holies from the rest
of the temple was rent from top to bottom. This showed that
God had acted. It was a sign from heaven. The way had been
opened for ordinary men and women to come directly to the
Lord God Almighty. No longer are God's people dependent
upon the high priest entering into the Most Holy Place once
a year for their sins. Now a new and living way has been
opened up for all of God's blood-bought people through

Christ's sacrifice at Calvary (Hebrews 10:19-20). Jesus said, 'I am the way' (John 14:6). Through his death, true Christians can come to God and he can come to them. The once-for-all sacrifice has been made to purchase access to God. Now the Lord dwells with his people. Christ has opened up the way to God.

The temple now

So where is the temple now? The Bible tells us that Jesus is the Temple of God. In John 2:19-21 the Jews were challenging the authority of Jesus, so he answered, '"Destroy this temple, and I will raise it again in three days." The Jews replied, "It has taken forty-six years to build this temple, and you are going to raise it in three days?" But the temple he had spoken of was his body.' The Jews had a tabernacle in the wilderness. This was a kind of tent used for religious purposes. John tells us in his Gospel that the Word of God (Jesus) has pitched his tent among us (John 1:14, literal translation). It is when we come to the Lord Jesus Christ in simple faith that we can come to God. How can that be possible? Because he dwells among us by his Spirit.

Then we read that the called-out people of God (the church) are now the temple of God. 'God has said: "I will live with them and walk among them, and I will be their God, and they will be my people' (2 Corinthians 6:16). It was the death of Christ that resulted in the 'supersession of the temple of Jerusalem, and his resurrection put another in its place'.[10]

The new temple is the body of Christ. The Christian community is now the temple of God, with Christ himself as the chosen and precious cornerstone (1 Peter 2:4-6). Each member of the church (i.e. the body of Christ) is, by virtue of being part of Christ's body, a temple of the Holy Spirit (1 Corinthians 6:19). Therefore all Christian believers have a solemn responsibility to live God-honouring lives because they, like the temple at Jerusalem in the time of Haggai, are the dwelling-place of the Lord Almighty.

There was only one temple, although it was rebuilt several times, and there is only one true church. Jesus Christ is the only foundation upon which the church can be built (see 1

Corinthians 3:9-17). And Jesus Christ is the only head of the church. He is called the chief cornerstone in Ephesians 2:20. It is Christ who holds the whole structure together. The church is not a temple made with hands (Acts 17:24), but it is a spiritual building still under construction. As people are being saved they are being joined to this building and 'In [to] him the whole building is joined together and rises to become a holy temple in the Lord' (Ephesians 2:21). Individual Christians must not live in isolation. They have a responsibility to this spiritual house of the Lord. 'And in him you too are being built together.' Why? 'To become a dwelling in which God lives by his Spirit' (Ephesians 2:22).

Peter takes the figure of the temple and shows how God's blood-bought people are brought into the house of God in order to be priests performing acts of worship. 'You also, like living stones, are being built into a spiritual house to be a holy priesthood, offering spiritual sacrifices acceptable to God through Jesus Christ' (1 Peter 2:5,9).

The new Jerusalem

Finally, think about the new Jerusalem. In Revelation 21, the Scriptures state that this will come down out of heaven from God, after the first heaven and earth have passed away (vv.1-2). But this new Jerusalem will have no temple in it (v.22). Why will there be no temple in the heavenly Jerusalem? Listen to the loud voice which will cry out from the throne, 'Now the dwelling of God is with men, and he will live with them. They will be his people, and God himself will be with them and be their God' (v.3). In verse 22 we also read that there will be no temple 'because the Lord God Almighty and the Lamb are its temple'. 'In a city modelled on the Holy of Holies there is no need of a temple; all is holy and God is everywhere adored.'[11]

2.
The reluctant builders

Message 1 (Part 1)
29 August 520 B.C.

Please read Haggai 1:1-2

Our spare room doubles as a sewing room. When any of my shirts, coats or pairs of trousers have buttons missing, all I have to do is leave them in the spare room and my wife will do the necessary repairs – when she gets time. I have, on occasions, been known to ask if a certain item of clothing has yet been mended. The reply I often get is something like, 'When you find time to put up the net curtains, I'll find time to sew on your buttons.'

We have many good intentions but finding the time is the problem. This was the trouble with the Jews who had returned from Babylon to their homeland. They intended to resume the rebuilding work in the temple but it had to be when the time was ripe, and that time had not yet arrived.

What time was it?

Haggai takes up this theme of time as he starts to deliver his first message. Time had been wasted as far as he was concerned. Time was passing quickly and nothing was being done to build up the house of God. It is amazing how Haggai was used by God to get things done. Some would say that he does not measure up to the greatness of Isaiah, Jeremiah or Ezekiel yet, in his own way, he achieved a task that these prophets did not do. They failed to prevent God's temple from being destroyed, because the people did not listen to their warnings. Yet Haggai had success. We know nothing about his beginnings or his death. We only know that he was so burdened by the complacency of the people that he did something about it. He did not come with great eloquence or superior wisdom (see 1 Corinthians 2:1); indeed his prophecy lacks the beautiful poetry of the 'great' prophets. But he had a real concern and he came at the right time, to the right place, and spoke the words that God had given to him.

Unlike many biblical prophecies his four messages are all dated, so we know the exact time when he delivered them. They were given between the end of August and the end of December in the year 520 B.C. (i.e. the second year of King Darius of Babylon).

Why were the Jews back in Judah?

Some eighteen years previously (in 538 B.C.) Cyrus, King of Persia, had decreed that all of his captive people should be allowed to return to their own lands if they wished and build temples to their gods. One of the tablets giving this order is on display in the British Museum. It is called the Cyrus Cylinder. You will find it in the middle of a display of similar objects in a room near the Egyptian mummies. Be careful that you don't miss it, as I nearly did! It only measures about nine inches in length. This remarkable find gives the gist of what is recorded in Ezra 1:2-4: 'This is what Cyrus king of Persia says: "The Lord, the God of heaven, has given me all the kingdoms of the earth and he has appointed me to build a temple for him at Jerusalem in Judah. Anyone of his people among you – may his God be with him, and let him go up to Jerusalem in Judah and build the temple of the Lord, the God of Israel, the God who is in Jerusalem. And the people of any place where survivors may now be living are to provide him with silver and gold, with goods and livestock, and with freewill offerings for the temple of God in Jerusalem."'

Almost as soon as the Jews arrived home they commenced work with great vigour. They located the site of the destroyed temple and rebuilt the altar. They celebrated the Feast of Tabernacles and reinstituted the system of regular burnt offerings (Ezra 3:1-6). Then they set about laying the foundations of the temple of the Lord: 'The priests in their vestments and with trumpets, and the Levites (the sons of Asaph) with cymbals, took their places to praise the Lord, as prescribed by David king of Israel. With praise and thanksgiving they sang to the Lord: "He is good; his love to Israel endures for ever'" (Ezra 3:10-11). At this the people gave a great shout of praise because the foundations of the house of the Lord had been laid.

Why did the work stop?

Why then was the work still unfinished in the year 520 B.C.? One of the reasons was because objections had arisen to the work of building the house. These arose not from heathen Babylon, in the first instance, but from the people who were already in the land. They came to the leaders of the Jews and said, 'Let us help you build because, like you, we seek your God and have been sacrificing to him since the time of Esarhaddon king of Assyria, who brought us here' (Ezra 4:2).

Zerubbabel, Joshua (who is called Jeshua throughout Ezra and Nehemiah) and the rest of the heads of the families of Israel lost no time in deciding what to do about this offer of help. They said, 'You have no part with us in building a temple to our God. We alone will build it for the Lord, the God of Israel, as King Cyrus, the king of Persia commanded us' (Ezra 4:3).

The Jews were jealous for the work of God's house. They recognized that only God's people can do God's work. Like Peter in Acts 8:21 they said, in effect, to this mixture of people (which probably included a large percentage of Samaritans), 'You have no part or share in this ministry, because your heart is not right before God.'

Why did the Jews have doubts about the sincerity of these people who already lived in the land? We are not told, but if these people really wanted to worship God in the Jerusalem temple why had they not made some prior attempt themselves to rebuild it? They showed their true colours when their help was refused. They 'took the huff'. Rather than helping, they set out to discourage the people of Judah and make them afraid to go on building. They hired counsellors to work against them and frustrate their plans during the entire reign of Cyrus king of Persia right down to the time of King Darius (Ezra 4:4-5).

Waiting for a convenient time

The sad thing was that their opposition to God's work proved
to be effective. During all these years the work just stopped.
Nothing else was done. Yet no one said, 'We've abandoned
this project.' They certainly intended to resume the rebuilding of the temple one day, but at a more convenient time.
They freely admitted that they had a duty to rebuild it. Indeed
this was the sole reason for their return from exile in Babylon
(Ezra 1:3). They were just waiting for the right moment to
take up the work again. They were waiting for a good opportunity, for more propitious times to arrive, for the task to
become easier. 'Meanwhile they became fat and comfortable
and middle-aged, while old ideals died.'[1] This is one of
Satan's subtlest temptations.

Enter God's servant

It is into this situation that this seemingly ordinary, but very
concerned servant of God, Haggai, comes to the fore.
Perhaps others, too, had been saddened by the state of
affairs, but it is through this man that God speaks.

To whom did Haggai go? He knew that the governor
Zerubbabel and the high priest Joshua were the ones who had
the responsibility for getting things done. The fact that they
were failing in their God-given task did not put off this determined man of God. He did not worry that these leaders
seemed to have had aristocratic forebears. Unlike Haggai,
their fathers' names are recorded.

What do we know about Zerubbabel? He appears in the
genealogies of our Lord in Matthew 1:12,13 and Luke 3:27
where he is described as the son of Shealtiel and grandson of
Neri. However, in 1 Chronicles 3:19 it is said that he is the son
of Pedaiah (brother of Shealtiel) and grandson of King
Jehoiachin. Wolf says that these complications are probably
due to the practice of levirate marriage and the differences
between legal and actual sons. 'Zerubbabel was probably the
natural son of Pedaiah and the legal son of Shealtiel. Similarly, Neri was most likely his natural grandfather, but child-
less King Jehoiachin enters the picture by adoption. Either

way, Zerubbabel is descended from David, whether through Solomon or Nathan, and this is the important point.'[2]

What was the relationship between Zerubbabel and Sheshbazzar? Many scholars believe that Zerubbabel took over the leadership from Sheshbazzar shortly after the Jews returned to their homeland but Theo Laetsch argues that these two names apply to the same person. He reminds us that the governor was called Sheshbazzar while he was in Babylon (Ezra 1:8,11; 5:14,16). He therefore concludes that this was his Babylonian name, because we know that Jews were given local names during the exile (see Daniel 1:6-7; Esther 2:7). He finds additional support for this view in Ezra 5. In verse 2 it is Zerubbabel who sets to work to rebuild the house of God at Jerusalem but verses 8-17 contain a letter written to King Darius (presumably in the Babylonian language and style), and in this letter the person who laid the foundations of the house of God in Jerusalem is called Sheshbazzar. Therefore, concludes Laetsch, these are one and the same person.[3]

It would appear that the governor and the high priest were godly men who were seeking to carry out the tasks laid upon them, but that they were affected by the lethargy that had fallen upon the whole of Judah. However, when Haggai joined them, things began to happen. Have you noticed what we have in verse 1? We have a prophet, the high priest and the governor (or ruler), all considering the word of the Lord. When these three combine is it not understandable that there should be a change for the better? Does this not remind you of our blessed Lord Jesus Christ? He is Prophet, Priest and King. His word must be obeyed in the minutest detail. No wonder that we read, 'The word of the Lord came.'

After more than a dozen years of reluctance to upset those who were opposing the work, God speaks. Then a dramatic improvement comes about.

The importance of the date

At what time did Haggai go to the leaders of the people? It was the first day of the sixth month of the reign of Darius. The first day of any month was the time of the appearing of the new moon. That meant it was a feast day for everyone. The farmers would be on holiday and all the workers would be resting. All business activities were suspended on feast days. They were like Sabbath days. It was an ideal time for people to have the leisure to listen to what God was saying to them. It was a time when, traditionally, people gathered to hear what the prophets of the Lord had to say.

Also notice that it was the sixth month. This meant that it followed the fifth month, which the Jews called by the name 'Ab', and which was the month in which Nebuchadnezzar had captured Jerusalem and levelled Solomon's temple. That had happened almost exactly sixty-seven years before Haggai commenced his work. It is interesting to note too, that Jews still gather at the Wailing Wall in the month of Ab to mourn the fall of Solomon's temple. Strangely, the second temple, beautified by King Herod, also fell in the month Ab. On this occasion it was the Romans who destroyed it (in A.D.70).

God's time had arrived

So we can see that this time was the time of God's choosing to stir up the people. They would have the opportunity to listen, they would be in a mood to receive God's Word and they were prepared for the solemnity of the hour.

There is a special phrase used to describe how the word of the Lord came. Verse 1 says, **'The word of the Lord came through the prophet Haggai'** (or 'by the hand of...'). The usual phrase we read in Scripture is 'The word of the Lord came *to*' Jeremiah, Ezekiel, Hosea etc., but here, and in the case of Malachi, 'the word of the Lord came *through*' them. God had something of the utmost importance to say. These two prophets were so in tune with God that the word of the Lord came through them.

Whose word was it?

It was the word of the Lord Almighty (A.V. 'Lord of hosts'). This description of God is never used in the Pentateuch but it appears more than eighty times in the post-exilic prophecies of Haggai, Zechariah and Malachi. It means 'Lord of armies'. In Isaiah 13:4 we read,

'Listen, a noise on the mountains,
  like that of a great multitude!
Listen, an uproar among the kingdoms,
  like nations massing together!
The Lord Almighty is mustering
  an army for war.'

This army may refer to angels, stars or the nation of Israel. God controls all of them and yet here in Haggai the all-powerful One speaks to a reluctant nation.

What does the Lord Almighty say?

'These people say, "The time has not yet come for the Lord's house to be built"' (1:2). Can you sense the disappointment in God's voice when he says 'these people'? He does not say 'my people'. He often does use that phrase, but not here. These people do not deserve to be spoken of in terms of God's ownership . By their disobedience, in putting their own comfort and wishes before the purposes of God, they have caused God to be angry. Because the people have persisted in their sins, for about sixteen years, God uses a term of reproach, as Jeremiah does in his prophecy: 'This is what the Lord says about this people:

"They greatly love to wander:
  they do not restrain their feet.
So the Lord does not accept them;
  he will now remember their wickedness
  and punish them for their sins'

(Jeremiah 14:10-11).

How does all this apply to us today?

The Jews knew that the reason why God had brought them to Jerusalem was to rebuild the temple. We have been placed in our situations by the Lord, not necessarily to erect a building made with hands but to build a church for God's glory. Yet we are reluctant to get on with the work. Perhaps we can learn a few important lessons by looking at some of the reasons why the work of rebuilding the temple had come to a standstill.

1. Opposition came

This came from the people who were already in the land. No one knows exactly who they were. We do know that when the Jews were taken away to Babylon, 'The commander left behind some of the poorest people of the land to work the vineyards and fields' (2 Kings 25:12). The King of Assyria then brought people from Babylon and other places to settle in the towns of Samaria (see 2 Kings 17:24-41). Perhaps some of these married those who had been left behind and this mixture of races and religions produced the Samaritans. The Jews were later to 'have no dealing with the Samaritans' (John 4:9 AV), mainly because of their corrupt religion. They only accepted the Pentateuch as the Word of God, they established their own priesthood and their own place of worship on Mount Gerazim. It is from here that their descendants still wait for the coming of the Messiah.[4]

So the people who frustrated the Jews in their attempts to rebuild the temple were probably of mixed race and mixed religion. They had not kept to the purity of the faith as had those who had been in the captivity in Babylon. They were upset because they could not bring their compromised religion and involve it in the rebuilding of the Lord's house. In Ezra 4:6-24 we read about how these people enlisted the help of the new king in Babylon by telling lies and getting the work stopped.

We should remember that we cannot, and we must not, compromise our faith. We should not be over-anxious about those who oppose the work of the Lord. We should be unafraid in our work for God. What God spoke to Zerubbabel long ago through Zechariah is still true today: '"This is the word of the Lord to Zerubbabel: 'Not by might nor by power, but by my Spirit,' says the Lord Almighty. What are you, O mighty mountain? Before Zerubbabel you will become level ground. Then he will bring out the capstone to shouts of 'God bless it! God bless it!'" Then the word of the Lord came to me: "The hands of Zerubbabel have laid the foundations of this temple; his hands will also complete it. Then you will know that the Lord Almighty has sent me to you. Who despises the day of small things? Men will rejoice when they see the plumb-line in the hand of Zerubbabel'" (Zechariah 4:6-10). How does one stand up to criticism and opposition? If you are in such a situation you should seek to be filled with the Holy Spirit and go out with a holy boldness to do the work of the Lord and endeavour to build his house.

2. The cost was too great

The people were poor. The harvests were bad (1:6) and those who had been ordered to supply money and materials (Ezra 1:4) had apparently failed to do so. Also those who had promised help had evidently not 'come up with the goods'.

This all made the Jews very frustrated. They were not able or not prepared to dig any deeper into their own pockets to finance the rebuilding programme. God's work sometimes flounders because his people are not prepared to make the necessary sacrifices to see that the work of the Lord's house makes progress. How many missionaries are unable to go out to the mission field because God's people have failed to give their tithes and offerings to his work? How many Christian workers are having to spend part of their time doing secular work in order to get enough for themselves and their families to live on because Christians are not facing up to their obligations to support them, and how many Christian charities are having to curtail their activities because they cannot afford to pay staff proper remuneration because the funds are being withheld by the Lord's people? Christians today, who have luxurious homes and possessions, often get 'hot under the collar' when giving to God's work is mentioned. 'Legalism' they say. 'You can't run the church on legalistic notions,' to which we reply, 'No, and you can't run it on hot air either.' God's work is being held up because God's people won't dig deeply enough into their pockets.

How we need to examine our hearts and our pockets to see whether we are guilty of hampering the Lord's work! Are our wallets and our cheque books fully consecrated to the Lord

and his work? Do we understand why God has given us
employment? It is not just so that we can spend our money as
we wish. We must remember to give the Lord's portion first.
If you are one of those people who say, 'Tithing is not a New
Testament principle,' just recall what Paul said immediately
after that great chapter on the resurrection: 'Now about the
collection for God's people: Do what I told the Galatian
churches to do. On the first day of every week, each one of
you should set aside a sum of money *in keeping with his
income*' (1 Corinthians 16:1-2). That means you should give
realistically, generously and cheerfully (2 Corinthians 9:7).

3. The people had grown weary in the work

This is the real reason why it stopped. Opposition often
causes God's work to grind to a halt, but think of Nehemiah.
He was not put off by similar opposition to his work. He built
the wall with a sword in one hand and a trowel in the other.
Think of Communist lands. There the church is often growing
quickly. Why does this happen where the gospel is severely
restricted, while in England, where we have religious
freedom, the work seems to founder? Have we lost our zeal
for the building of God's house?

   The people had become lethargic. They had 'become weary
in doing good' (see Galatians 6:9). They had lost sight of the
Lord's glory. Their vision had grown dim, and we are told that
'Where there is no vision, the people perish' (Proverbs 29:18
AV). Do we have a vision for the presence and glory of God
among us? Do we want his glory to be displayed in the neighbourhood where we work and witness for God? Let us smash
our lethargic spirit into smithereens and rise up to build for
God's glory.

4. They had become discouraged

Not everyone was pulling their weight. Some had started
well, but then they got fed up and eventually stopped
altogether. Those of us who are older Christians should be
very careful about our attitude to the Lord's work because
others are taking the lead from us. When mature Christians
slacken in the building up of God's house, weaker and newer

Christians often find that they reduce their efforts too. They may even give up altogether, as these Jews did.

The people of Judah became disillusioned. They had not seen results quickly enough. They lacked the determination to press ahead. They had given up, at least for the time being. Are we like this when it comes to the work of the Lord's house, for example in the work of prayer? Do we give up praying if we apparently get few answers to our prayers? Let us not be like these Jews who in their discouragement had said, 'We'll give it a rest for a while.' Sixteen years or so had drifted by and they were still saying, 'The time has not yet come for the Lord's house to be built.' Let us not give up in the work of the kingdom. Let us work and wrestle in prayer and every other way for the glory of God's house.

5. They were too busy

The harvests were very poor (Haggai 1:6) and all their energies were going into growing and gathering food. Much of their time needed to be spent in getting every last ounce out of the land. Times were hard, and when there are difficulties self so often comes to the fore. The spirit of the world gets into us. The important thing seems to be that we must earn more and more money on every possible occasion. This is not so that we can give more to the work of God, but so that we can maintain our own standards of living, 'keeping up with the Joneses next door'. Prayer must wait. We are too busy to go regularly to the house of God. We are too tired to attend the church prayer meetings or take part in evangelistic outreach programmes. We stop going to the evening service and soon a Sunday morning lie-in becomes vital! No wonder we are failing to engage in the urgent rebuilding of God's house! Because we are too tired and too busy with other things, we are sheltering behind the delusion that 'The time has not yet come for the Lord's house to be rebuilt.'

6. They may have had a wrong view of prophecy

Both Daniel and Jeremiah had prophesied that Jerusalem would be desolate for seventy years (Jeremiah 25:11; Daniel 9:1-2). All the people knew these prophecies but they had not heeded the warnings given by the prophets, and so they had to suffer the captivity in Babylon. As a result of their sin, Jerusalem had lain waste for many years. Surely their consciences must have been pricked on occasions because they were not getting on with the rebuilding work that God had called them to do when they returned to Judah. They may well have tried to salve their consciences by saying, 'Oh, it's all right. There are still several years to go before seventy years have passed since Jerusalem was destroyed. We can't do anything about prophecy. It's written and we must wait until the full seventy years of desolation have elapsed.'

Don't we often reason like that? Biblical prophecy becomes a hobby. We think that we know all the answers. We get out all our Bible charts covered with dates, the names of kings and prophets and long Greek words, and say, 'The time hasn't yet arrived for God to work.'

The lethargic Jews had assumed that the seventy years began with the fall of Jerusalem, when in fact it may well have begun two or three years earlier when Nebuchadnezzar's armies first set up their siege of the holy city. Let us confess to the Lord that we do not know all the answers to prophecy. Let us seek for his illumination and his guidance in our work for him and for his glory. And let us never use the excuse that there is plenty of time before we need to start building for God's glory. May our prayer be 'It is time O Lord for you to work.'

3.
The selfish builders

Message 1 (Part 2)
29 August 520 B.C.

Please read Haggai 1:3-11

Many times during the 1987 general election we were exhorted to consider the benefits of the higher standard of living which the country was then enjoying. We were told about the increased wealth and the greater number of possessions we could all have if only we worked harder and invested our money wisely.

The remnant of God's people who had returned from the captivity in Babylon were also hard workers. They wasted no time in idle speculation but engaged energetically in the activities that were necessary for the well-being of their nation. They reasoned that if they put all their energies into the accumulation of wealth and good things, then one day they would be in a suitable position to be able to resume the work of rebuilding the temple of God in Jerusalem. They knew that was why they had been restored to their homeland. They acknowledged that God was with them in their desire to re-establish a godly state in the old southern kingdom of Judah, and they recognized that this building work must be carried out. However, they did want the temple to be fit for God's presence. They probably feared that heathen nations would laugh at them if, in their haste, they erected a building which was inferior to the temples of the gods of the heathen peoples. At the right time they would get around to building a house suitable for God's glory.

Haggai's challenge

This is probably how they were feeling on that August day in 520 B.C. when Haggai stormed up to Zerubbabel and Joshua (as Elijah had earlier rushed in to see King Ahab, 1 Kings 17:1). The prophet of God shattered their complacency by his biting words: **'Is it a time for you yourselves to be living in your panelled houses, while this house remains a ruin?'** (1:3).

We do not know exactly what condition the temple was in, only that it was in ruins. It had been destroyed by fire by Nebuchadnezzar's armies and Haggai describes it as a 'ruin' (1:4,9). This desolation shocked Haggai. He could not understand how God's people could live in Jerusalem without making some attempt to rebuild the temple. Calvin points out that the people probably reasoned that their fathers had lived many years without a temple so God must be satisfied with what was happening. 'There's now an altar erected, and there sacrifices are offered...[but] they built not even a tent for God and sacrificed in the open air.'[1]

We can be sure that some of the people must have had a conscience about this sad state of affairs, but we can be certain too that, like us, they rationalized their way out of their dilemma. 'No, we should not start to build anything without first counting the cost,' they probably said. Perhaps they even knew Psalm 127! 'We can't go rushing into things without making careful and detailed plans,' was another variation on the same excuse. They certainly reasoned, 'We are not yet wealthy enough.'

An urgent problem

They had an urgent problem on their hands. The harvest had failed (1:6). They needed good harvests in order to live. There were some 50,000 of them and there were no supermarkets down the road! The people who had lived in the land during their absence were weak, disorganized and few in number. They could not depend upon them to sell them food or provide for their needs. The only way the Jews could survive was by the good use of agriculture, so they worked hard on the land. They were not lazy. They knew their continued existence depended upon a successful harvest. They tilled the land well. They had the advantage of knowing that it ought to produce a bumper crop because most of it had lain fallow for some sixty-seven years.

This meant that the minerals had had time to build up in the soil. After all, this was the promised land and 'flowing with milk and honey'; surely they would be successful if only they worked hard and treated the land in the correct way!

The Jews were expectant. They had done the right thing in the right way and now they were waiting for the reward for their labours. But it turned out to be **'little'** (1:9). Their expectations of a good harvest had not materialized. Look at verse 6. The food they ate did not satisfy their hunger. The liquid they drank did not slake their thirst. The clothes they wore did not keep them warm and the wages they earned did not last long or buy what they wanted. They were in a sad state. Things had not come up to their expectations. They were a discontented people and the reason they were not satisfied was because of their selfish desires.

These Jews 'expected much' for the wrong reason. It was not that they wanted much so that they could give abundantly to provide for the rebuilding expenses; it was so that they could satisfy their own cravings for more and greater material possessions. Their expectations were great, like those of William Carey when he preached his famous sermon in 1792 entitled 'Expect great things from God and attempt great things for God,' but they did not attempt the great things. They expected the blessing but they were not prepared to put spiritual exertion into their labours. Jesus was later to sum it up perfectly when he preached the Sermon on the Mount. He spoke of those with little faith and said, 'Do not worry, saying, "What shall we eat?" or "What shall we drink?" or "What shall we wear?" For the pagans run after all these things, and your heavenly Father knows that you need them. But *seek first his kingdom and his righteousness,* and all these things will be given to you as well. Therefore do not worry about tomorrow, for tomorrow will worry about itself. Each day has enough trouble of its own' (Matthew 6:31-33).

The cause of their poor harvests

It did not seem to them that it was their fault. They had done everything that they should have done. They had expectations of a good harvest. They had prepared the ground well.

They had worked hard. Their fault was not that they had
failed to sow the seed correctly, but their wrong attitude.
Haggai said that God was speaking to them through their
poor harvests. It was the Lord Almighty who had sent this
punishment. He had done this in order to bring them to their
senses. God said, **'I called for a drought'** (1:11). And when
God calls, nature listens and obeys.

In hot lands the dew is almost as plentiful and important as
rain. It falls each night and nourishes the corn, stopping it
from becoming scorched under the hot sun. During this particular harvest-time even the dew failed to reach the crops
(1:10). God is sovereign. He can order rain to come or to be
withheld. In Bible lands rain is so important to agriculture. It
is a sign of God's blessing or his disapproval. He had often
said that he would punish the people by withholding rain from
the earth. 'If...you will not listen to me, I will punish you for
your sins seven times over. I will break down your stubborn
pride and make the sky above you like iron and the ground
beneath you like bronze. Your strength will be spent in vain,
because your soil will not yield its crops, nor will the trees of
the   land   yield   their   fruit'   (Leviticus   26:18-20;   cf.
Deuteronomy 28:23-24).

What happened when God stopped the rain and dew from
falling? Look at verse 11. The fields became dry and parched
and produced little. The mountains stopped supplying
streams of water. The grain did not swell on its stalk. The
grapes, when squeezed, did not make much new wine. (The
old wine had probably almost run out.) The olives failed to
provide sufficient oil for cooking, lighting and heating and
medicinal needs. The ground produced nothing of much
value. Men and cattle died of thirst and all the work of the
farm labourers led to failure.

Why did God send this punishment?

It was because the people had a wrong attitude towards God
and his glory. They said to themselves, 'There is plenty of
time to honour God. There's plenty of time to do what he
wants. There's plenty of time to please him.' They said, in
effect, 'Let us put ourselves first.' More than anything else,

they wanted blessing for themselves and their families. This all sounds a very laudable objective, but when self is put on the throne then someone else must be pushed to one side.

'Do you want blessing?' says God. 'Well, not until you change your attitude to me, and my work, will blessing again begin to come upon you.'

The selfishness of the Jews

God sent punishment because the Jews thought only of their own needs, not of building up the temple of God. This is the crux of the whole matter. They had used all their energy and resources in building, not God's temple, but fine houses for themselves: **'Each of you is busy with his own house'** (1:9). The Authorized Version translates this, 'Ye run every man to his own house.' The words 'busy' and 'run' convey the idea of tremendous activity *about their own dwelling-places*.

Think what they had done. They said, 'Before we can make a start on God's house, we need places to live in ourselves.' This was very plausible reasoning, and God does not punish them for wanting houses. He realizes that people work better if they have reasonably comfortable and warm places to sleep in. What God was complaining about was their extravagance. This is why Haggai passed on God's message in verse 3: **'Is it a time for you yourselves to be living in your panelled houses, while this house remains a ruin?'**

'Panelled' can be translated 'cieled' (AV) or 'vaulted-roofed'. The point is that they were living in luxurious homes, while God's house lay in ruins. Where did they get the timber to make the panelling for the walls and roofs of their houses? We do not know, but it is not beyond the realms of possibility that they 'borrowed' it from the stocks of timber that had been amassed for the temple when the Jews first returned from exile.

The Jews had been sent back to Palestine for the express purpose of building up the temple of the Lord but, instead, they had built up their own houses. Instead of spending time, effort and money on God's house they had used all these things for building up their own homes. As well as being disobedient to God, they were guilty of robbing him (cf. Malachi 3:8). What is more, they had no conscience about these

things, unlike King David many years before. He had said,
'Here I am, living in a palace of cedar, while the ark of God
remains in a tent' (2 Samuel 7:2).

Why then, was there a drought? God gives the answer himself. He says it is **'because of my house, which remains a ruin,
while each of you is busy with his own house'**. He makes a play
on the words 'desolate' and 'drought'. In Hebrew these two
words are spelt the same, with the exception of one tiny vowel
sign. It is as though God was saying, 'Right then, you were
content to leave my house *desolate* (1:4,9). Now I will give
you a taste of your own medicine and see how you like it. I will
send you a *drought.*' God goes on to underline his displeasure
by saying in verse 10 that all this is **'because of you'**. 'You
thought you could save money by not yet building the temple.
You thought you could gain more cash by putting your effort
into farming. Well, I'm teaching you that obedience to my
commands is the only real way to success in material and in
spiritual life.'

What can we learn from this passage?

God has called us to be active in building up his temple, the
church of Jesus Christ (Ephesians 2:19-22). This is a very solemn and challenging task. Do we measure up to it or are we
too busy about our own affairs? Haggai calls us, as he called
the selfish builders of 520 B.C., to **'give careful thought to
[our] ways'** (1:5,7; 2:15,18).

We need to consider what God is saying to us today. Like
the Jews of Haggai's time we find that we 'earn wages' only to
put them in a purse with holes in it (1:6). God is speaking to
us through the daily circumstances of our life. He is saying to
us, as they say in Lancashire, 'Think on'.[2]

Have you come before the Lord and considered what he is
saying to you through the things that are happening to you
and around you? When trouble comes, have you ever said to
God, 'You are sending – or allowing this – in order to teach
me something. What is it, Lord? Help me to listen to what you
are saying and put it into practice'?

We are good at blaming other people for what is wrong with
the country, the town, the family and the church. We even try

to blame God sometimes when things go wrong. Now stop and 'think on'. Is there anything wrong in your life which is displeasing to God and is holding up his work? Are you a hindrance to the building up of Christ's church? When you have found out what is wrong confess it to God and seek to repent of it.

God is saying to us all, 'Are you living in panelled houses, while my house remains a ruin?' In other words, 'Are you more concerned about your comforts than the welfare of the kingdom of God?' How we need to confess our selfishness in regard to our possessions! Jesus said, 'A man's life does not consist in the abundance of his possessions' (Luke 12:15). It is not *what* you possess that matters but *who* you possess, or rather who possesses you.

The more we have, the more we want. The most wealthy people in the world seem to find life a great trial. Possessions do not necessarily bring happiness. It is when we are relaxing in plenty that Satan creeps in unawares and leads away from God. 'Better a little with the fear of the Lord than great wealth with turmoil' (Proverbs 15:16).

Some of the most contented people in the world are those who own few material possessions. 'The more we learn to do without, the richer we will feel with what we have, because our wants will be less. Christian plainness and simplicity of life is therefore the answer to today's affluent society.'[3] Paul learnt, even in his imprisonment, that the secret of success is being 'content in any and every situation, whether well fed or hungry, whether living in plenty or in want' (Philippians 4:12). He also wrote that 'Godliness with contentment is great gain' (1 Timothy 6:6).

God is in control. We may think we can keep him waiting and delay our obedience to his commands, but he will make us listen and compel us to obey him. There is not plenty of time to do what God wants us to do. Time is quickly passing. These Jews were obsessed with time and they concluded that there was plenty of it. God has given us this wonderful commodity of time. It only comes once and it can never be recalled. How do we use it?

God will bring about his purposes despite our delays. God is the powerful Creator and sustainer of the universe. The old hymn says,

Sovereign ruler of the skies,
Ever gracious, ever wise;
All my times are in thy hand,
All events at thy command.

(Ryland)

God's sovereignty displayed itself in these Jews because, a few weeks after Haggai first spoke to the governor and high priest about the desolation of the Lord's house, things began to happen.

4.
The obedient builders

Message 1 (Part 3)
21 September 520 B.C.

Please read Haggai 1:12-15

God sometimes shocks us into obedience. It seems as though all of the people who had returned from the Babylonian exile were drifting along quite nicely. It was true that not everything had gone smoothly for them but, by and large, they were managing to 'get by'. Everyone meant to do the right thing. No one really forgot that God had been gracious to them. He had brought them home to build up the temple so that God's glory could again be seen throughout the land. And that is what they intended to do – one day!

They were enjoying their freedom and pretending that everything was all right when Haggai arrived and shattered their complacency. They did not want to be told that God's blessing had been withdrawn from them. Life was hard enough without being reminded of their religious duty to rebuild the house of the Lord. However, they had to admit that the harvests had been abysmal failures. Inflation was so bad that it appeared they were putting their wages in pockets which had holes in them, or purses which had no bottoms, and they suspected that God had turned his back upon them.

'Give careful thought to your ways' (1:5,7) was truly what they ought to do. Haggai's message was making them think. They thought deeply about their lives and began to pray, and as they thought and prayed they started to tremble. When God sent his prophet Haggai among the people with the message of the Lord, things began to happen. God's Spirit was at work among them and they were discomforted. More than that, they were stirred up to action!

The leaders took the initiative

Someone had to do something. 'Had there been no leaders, no one of the common people would have pointed out the way to the rest. We know what usually happens when a word is addressed indiscriminately to all the people: they wait for one another.'[1] Verse 12 starts with the word 'then'. It was when all the people had been reminded of their duty and the chastisement of God upon them that **'Zerubbabel son of Shealtiel, Joshua son of Jehozadak, the high priest, and the whole remnant of the people obeyed the voice of the Lord their God.'**

Rarely in the records of prophecy has such a short message received such a rapid and dramatic response. Zerubbabel and Joshua, the leaders to whom the prophet first spoke in verse 1, are appropriately the first to respond. Normally, where these two men are referred to in the same verse, Zerubbabel's office as governor of Judah is also mentioned (1:1,14; 2:2) but here, in verse 12 and in 2:4 the title is omitted. Wolf suggests that perhaps 'Zerubbabel is not responding as governor but as an individual who needs to repent.'[2] Joshua, however, is called 'son of Jehozadak, the high priest,' and this full title is used consistently whenever Joshua is mentioned in Haggai.

The remnant

The people were included too. They are called **'the whole remnant of the people'**. This term is also used for the returned exiles in 1:14 and 2:2. It is the word describing the whole company of the Jews who had been restored to their land. They are also called this in Zechariah 8:6,11,12.

In everyday life we usually associate the term remnant with the short lengths of cloth which are sold off cheaply in fabric shops or on market stalls. These are the pieces which are left over at the end of a roll of material when most of it has been sold. A remnant is something left over from a much larger amount. The 'rest' and the 'remainder' are similar terms for the same idea.

The theme of the remnant had been especially characteristic

of Isaiah's prophecy. In the temple vision Isaiah was warned of destruction, which only a small proportion would survive (Isaiah 6:11-13), and the name of his son, Shear-Jashub (meaning 'a remnant shall return') became a *motif* in his preaching (Isaiah 7:3; 10:21; 11:11). The prophet Micah also used the word 'remnant' to describe the faithful few within the nation (Micah 5:7,8).

However, the Jews were not God's faithful remnant merely because of their physical presence in the land. More was required of them if they were to fulfil Isaiah's hopes. They needed to repent of their sin. Two months later Zechariah was to say to these same people, 'This is what the Lord Almighty says: "Return to me," declares the Lord Almighty, "and I will return to you" (Zechariah 1:3). The verb translated 'return' also means 'repent' and 'It is significant that in Haggai the word 'remnant' is applied to them *when they respond in obedience* to the voice of the Lord their God.'[3]

God's people today are a remnant

Those who are trying to obey God's Word and put it into practice in these days are the faithful remnant. So many who think of themselves as God's people are just asleep to God's voice. They will not stir themselves to leave their 'Babylon'. They are comfortable in their surroundings. They are not bothered by the ungodliness of their associates. They see no need to obey the call to 'come out from them and be separate' (2 Corinthians 6:17).

But the remnant today are characterized by a concern to listen carefully to God's Word and a desire to apply it to their church and personal lives. They are not happy to allow the thinking and desires of the ungodly world to dominate their lives and their Christian fellowships. They are concerned to maintain a purity of doctrine in their churches and they want to do all they can to follow the teaching of the Word of God. Above all, they repent deeply of their past complacency and endeavour to place God's Word at the centre of their thoughts and actions.

The one sent by God

It had been many years since there had been a prophet among God's people. Perhaps there had been false prophets who had tried to persuade the people to follow wrong teaching, but Haggai was a true prophet of God. He spoke with the voice of God. He had been sent by the Lord and the people recognized the authenticity of his office and his word. As a result, they **'obeyed the voice of the Lord their God and the message of the prophet Haggai'**. Why did they do this? **'Because the Lord their God had sent him.'**

What made the message of Haggai authentic? It was because he spoke God's word. Calvin says that 'We know that men are not sent by divine authority to speak that God himself may be silent.'[4] Prophets are recognized because they speak the truth, they honour God, they uphold his word, they are concerned about his glory and the Holy Spirit stirs up the people as a result of their preaching.

The people took notice of the message

The remnant accepted the challenge of God's word through his servant. For the previous twenty-three days they had been giving careful thought to their ways. They made no hasty decision; to consider something carefully takes time. If they tried to immerse themselves in work or pleasure they still could not get the word of the Lord out of their minds. They were serious about what God was saying to them.

They considered their lives and they saw they were neglecting God's house. They realized that they were spending more time and effort on their own things than on the things of God. As a result of Haggai's words they had to make a decision. No doubt they were somewhat annoyed by this prophet, Haggai. What right had he got to come and try to shake them out of the comfortable rut they were in? They did not want to be reminded about God's Word. They wanted to carry on with their own affairs and keep God shut away in a small corner of their lives.

But, having thought carefully about their life-style, they realized that they had to take God's word seriously. This meant acknowledging that they were behaving selfishly by living in their comfortable homes, while God's house was a ruin. They had to admit that they had sinned against the holiness of God. They needed to undergo a painful repentance, and they cast themselves upon God's mercy.

So they put aside any prejudices they may have had against Haggai, and listened to what he had to say. They recognized that God was speaking to them, and their own situation. They listened to the prophet, acknowledging that it was the voice of God that they were hearing.

As they listened to Haggai the people recognized that he added nothing of his own to the message and no one quibbled with his authority to speak to them in this way. They all acknowledged that it was not just the voice of a man they were hearing but that the Lord Almighty himself was speaking to them (1:2,5,7). When such a powerful God speaks he is a foolish man who refuses to listen. No wonder we read of the effect of the message: **'Then Zerubbabel...Joshua...and...the people obeyed.'**

The people feared the Lord

What does it mean to fear the Lord? It means to reverence him, to have a holy awe and respect for God. It means to acknowledge that God is supreme and the one in control of all events. The one who reverences the Lord is not apathetic to God's voice or the voice of his 'sent servants'.

When a people fear the Lord they have a desire to please him. When anyone truly loves God there is something wrong if they do not want to please him. And pleasing God is always shown by obedience. Abraham proved that he feared God when he willingly offered Isaac on the altar of sacrifice, thus obeying the voice of God (Genesis 22:12,18). To fear the Lord is to love him more than oneself or one's family. To fear the Lord is to love him and obey him with whole-hearted devotion. When people have a holy fear of God they are acting wisely. 'The fear of the Lord is the beginning of wisdom' (Psalm 111:10).

'Instead of shrinking from their task for fear of hostile neighbours, the returned exiles began to fear the one whose power was far greater. They had a new awe, a new reverence for the God who shakes heaven and earth and overthrows kingdoms and nations (2:6,22).'[5]

The people obeyed the Lord

When they were living in disobedience God had called them 'these people' (1:2). God is displeased when his people are disobedient. Disobedience always cuts off God's people from his blessing but despite that, God is still the Father of his people and they are still his children. The problem is that there is something wrong with the relationship. There is a barrier which has caused a separation between God and his people. For these people it was in their daily lives. Their crops did not grow. The money they had was not sufficient for their needs. The awareness of the presence of God had become blurred. This sin of disobedience needed to be dealt with before a proper relationship could be restored between God and his wayward people.

However, when the people listened to the voice of the Lord their God, and their listening issued forth in obedience, a dramatic change took place. Haggai now refers to the Lord as **'their God'** (twice in verse 12 and again in verse 14). This change comes about as soon as the people show that they intend to obey God and resume work on the temple.

God is very gracious. He does not wait, as a terrible frightening ogre might lurk in the shadows, until his people actually achieve what they say they are going to do. He looks at the heart. He sees their intentions and he is satisfied. He then refers to them as his own children.

God was with them

Immediately after their resolve to obey God, Haggai gave the rest of the Lord's message to the people. He gave them a wonderful promise. He said, **'I am with you'** (1:13). The presence of God is what makes all the difference. When they obeyed God in their hearts, they were given the promise of God's presence, and the promise is sufficient for them. The promise is reality. It is God's word and he never breaks his promise. He is so unlike human beings; what he says, he will do. He has the ability and the will to carry out his word.

Who is with them? It is the Lord Almighty. This is the same God who had ever been with his people. When Jacob had to go back to Canaan, he was afraid of his brother Esau, but God gave him a wonderful promise. He said, 'Go back to the land of your fathers and to your relatives, and *I will be with you*' (Genesis 31:3).

This same God was with Moses when he was confronted with the burning bush. God told him to go back into Egypt. Naturally he was scared because he had made a hurried exit from that land many years before. He had killed an Egyptian and the knowledge of his deed had become known. What did God tell Moses? *'I will be with you'* (Exodus 3:12).

This wonderful God was the one who promised to lead the people through the difficulties and the dangers of the wilderness. He said to Moses, *'My Presence will go with you,* and I will give you rest' (Exodus 33:14).

Later on, when the people were afraid to go into the promised land, because there were giants in it, Joshua and Caleb said to them, 'Do not rebel against the Lord. And do not be afraid of the people of the land, because we will swallow them up. Their protection is gone, but *the Lord is with us*. Do not be afraid of them' (Numbers 14:9).

When Joshua had the awesome task of taking over from Moses the leadership of the children of Israel, he was naturally very apprehensive. Not only were they largely an untrained rabble but he had to lead them into Canaan and conquer many hostile cities and tribes before he could gain possession of the land. But God said, 'As I was with Moses, so *I will be with you;* I will never leave you nor forsake you' (Joshua 1:5).

In Isaiah 43:1-2 we read that God said to his people,

> 'Fear not, for I have redeemed you;
>   I have summoned you by name; you are mine.
> When you pass through the waters,
>   *I will be with you;*
> and when you pass through the rivers,
>   they will not sweep over you.'

Also in verse 5 of the same chapter God says, 'Do not be afraid, for *I am with you.*'

Also in Isaiah 7:14 we read of a wonderful child who will be born to a virgin. His name is to be 'Immanuel' which means, *'God is with us.'*

Think of what all of this must have meant to these Jews. They knew their history. They knew the promises of the past. Could this same almighty God be with them also? If they were to know his presence with them personally then they would realize that they were no longer cut off from the Lord. The same mighty God who had delivered them from all their enemies in the past was with them in the same powerful way, to meet the demands of the present and also the future.

The evidence of God's presence

What happened because the Lord of hosts was with them? They were stirred up in their spirits (1:14). Something was happening to them. Just as God had mightily moved in the hearts of the Jews eighteen years before (Ezra 1:5), so once again God moved in them and they set to work, at long last, to rebuild the house of the Lord.

Do you realize that it had only taken twenty-three days from the time Haggai had first spoken (1:2) to the time they resumed their rebuilding programme? That was obedience indeed!

What had taken place during those twenty-three days? During that short time they had worked hard. They had stirred up the rest of the Jews to work. They had quickly finished off gathering their meagre harvest. (The sixth month was the month of harvesting.) They had gone up to the mountains to cut, trim and carry down much precious timber and they had sorted out the building materials which had lain rotting for the past sixteen years.

They had been busily engaged in preparing to build the temple of the Lord; and on the twenty-fourth day of the sixth month of the second year of King Darius, **'They came and began work on the house of the Lord Almighty their God'** (1:14-15).

God speaks to us today

God speaks in different ways but it is always God's Word which is powerful, not man's. God is speaking to us through what is happening in the world today. He speaks through what is happening in our neighbourhood, in our churches and in our own lives and circumstances.

We need to take God's Word seriously. We need to stop listening to anything which takes our minds off what God is saying to us today. Do we use Radio One as background noise? Do we hate missing *The Eastenders* or *Dallas* or one of its offspring? We should ask ourselves, 'Do these other voices stop me listening to God's authentic voice and are their moral standards speaking ever more clearly to my heart?'

In these days anyone can preach; everyone who cannot think of a good reason why they should not do it is forced into taking a Sunday School class, and the note of the authentic prophet has been cheapened by the way in which all kinds of people can give a 'prophecy' in a meeting. How can we tell whether we are hearing a true servant of God? We must ask ourselves, 'Is this person speaking the word of God? Does his message tie in with the whole of the teaching of God's Word? Is the Holy Spirit stirring up the hearts of the people to obey the voice of God?'

These Jews obeyed the voice of the Lord their God *and* the message of the prophet Haggai because they recognized that **'the Lord their God had sent him'**. We may not like what we hear from our teachers and preachers. We may not think the preacher is very eloquent, but we must listen for the voice of God, wherever that voice is proceeding from and whoever the speaker might be.

We live in days where easy access to God seems to mean that people can have an irreverent approach to our Lord when they address him in prayer. If we really lived our lives in the fear of the Lord we would have a ready obedience to his commands. We seem to have lost the vision of the holiness and splendour of our great God. We have little of the attitude of Isaiah in Isaiah 6 or John in Revelation 1. How we need to confess our flippancy and listen to God and obey him! For the

Hebrews 'listening to the voice of the Lord' is the normal idiom for obeying the Lord.

At the end of Matthew's Gospel, when Jesus was bidding farewell to his disciples just before he ascended into heaven, he said to them, 'Go and make disciples of all nations, baptizing them in the name of the Father and of the Son and of the Holy Spirit, and teaching them *to obey everything I have commanded you.* And surely I am with you always, to the very end of the age' (Matthew 28:19-20).

Have you considered your ways? Have you acknowledged that all is not right in your life and in the life of your church fellowship, and that you need to confess and repent of your sins? Have you obeyed *everything* that God has commanded you?

Listen carefully and prayerfully to God's Word, desire to obey him and he will stir you up by his Spirit to serve the living God. Don't just sit there. Get on and obey God.

5.
The discouraged builders

Message 2
17 October 520 B.C.

Please read Haggai 2:1-9

Less than a month had gone by since the Jews had started to rebuild the temple and already they were beginning to feel 'fed up'; their enthusiasm for the work was starting to flag. They had commenced work with a will. They had grasped the vision of building a temple for God's glory. They had been stirred up in their spirits and had begun 'work on the house of the Lord Almighty, their God, on the twenty-fourth day of the sixth month in the second year of King Darius' (1:14-15). But now their zeal was beginning to diminish, so God sent Haggai to them a second time.

The prophet delivered four messages in all to the returned exiles, each of which was dated. In the first one he spoke sharply in order to urge them to obey God's clear command. Now, and in the subsequent two messages, Haggai speaks gently, using words of encouragement. He begins his second message (2:1-9) in a similar way to the start of his earlier one. He reflects what the people were thinking. In 1:2 they said, 'The time has not yet come to build the temple.' Now in 2:3 he repeats what the people were complaining about: 'The temple we are rebuilding is not as glorious as Solomon's.' They were discouraged. Why?

1. The state of the temple site

One of the less enjoyable aspects of wallpapering is the great length of time which has to be spent preparing the surfaces of the walls. Even getting ready to decorate a house which has been empty for some while bears no comparison to the vast amount of work which these Jews needed to do to get the temple site ready for building. God's house had been utterly destroyed and burnt to the ground by Nebuchadnezzar (2 Kings 25:9; 2 Chronicles 36:19). On top of this destruction sixty-six years of neglect had taken their toll. Before a start could be made on rebuilding the temple, a great deal of rubbish had to be removed.

This rubble had piled up high. It was like one of those ugly bomb-sites that were all over London during and just after the last war. By 520 B.C. weeds and brambles had been growing all over the fallen masonry blocks for many years. Naturally, much of these initial three and a half weeks had been taken up with clearing the ground. Remember, the Jews had none of today's mechanical aids to help them, so the rubbish took ages to clear away. When they started the rebuilding pro- gramme all of them were keen. Now the heavy spadework was beginning to dampen their zeal.

2. The continual stream of delays

They had started off enthusiastically, knowing that they were obeying God's commands. But religion got in the way. They frequently had to stop for sacred rest days, and this was begin- ning to cause irritation.

Every week there was a Sabbath day. No one could do any work on these seventh days, and there had already been three of them since they had started to rebuild. Then the Feast of Trumpets had occurred on the first day of that particular month (the seventh month). Again this was a whole day when no work could be done. On the tenth day of the month the sol- emn Day of Atonement fell. Again on the fifteenth day the week-long Festival of Booths, or Tabernacles, began. During this feast period the whole population moved out of their houses to live in leafy shelters. This is still done today (climate permitting) to remind the Jews of their wanderings in the wil- derness following the exodus from Egypt. No wonder the people began to think that religious observances were a nuisance. They were holding up the important rebuilding programme.

Furthermore the Festival of Booths had become linked

with a time of thanksgiving for God's provision of the harvest.
Jews remembered, at this festival, God's faithfulness to his
promise that

> 'As long as the earth endures,
> seedtime and harvest,
> cold and heat,
> summer and winter,
> day and night
> will never cease'

(Genesis 8:22).

As these builders, during their time of enforced idleness,
gave thanks to God for his bountiful provision they must have
reflected that the harvest in 520 B.C. had been so poor that
they hardly felt like spending much time celebrating it (1:6).

3. The shortage of resources

They had none of the wealth that had gone into King Solomon's temple. When the first temple had been built there
was an abundance of material waiting to be used. Although
King David had been forbidden by God to build a temple
himself, he had not been idle. He had spent much time
gathering together fabric for the building. And then,
remember that King Solomon himself was also a wealthy
man. He had many mines which yielded precious metals and
he had much money with which to buy timber from Lebanon.
What had Zerubbabel got as he started on the rebuilding
work? Hardly anything!

Not only were the Jews of 520 B.C. poorly off for materials,
they also lacked the craftsmen who had the necessary skills to
perform such a tremendous task as rebuilding the temple for
God's glory. What had happened to all the Jewish craftsmen?
Many of them had perished during the years of exile in
Babylon. Perhaps some of the trades had died out altogether
and many of the skills had been lost through lack of use.

The Jews became discouraged further when they considered God's plans for the rebuilt temple. What had the
prophets said? They had spoken of a future temple which

would be far more glorious than Solomon's temple. Isaiah and Jeremiah had prophesied of a marvellous house of God (e.g. Isaiah 60) and Ezekiel had even described it in great detail (Ezekiel 40-43). No wonder the people became discouraged when they realized that their efforts were puny and the end result would be far, far inferior to Solomon's temple.

4. The missing elements

In Solomon's temple there had been elements which were now absent.

1. The sacred fire

This had formerly come down from heaven and consumed the animal sacrifices.

2. The Shekinah

This was the glory, the divine presence 'represented by a visible appearance, or given, as it were to the king and high-priest, by anointing with the oil of unction'.[1]

3. The ark and cherubim

God gave his answers from these by a clear and audible voice.

4. The Urim and Thummin

The high priest was miraculously instructed about the will of God by these mysterious objects.

5. The spirit of prophecy

This was given to those who were especially called to the prophetic office.

Encouragement at the festival

It was on the twenty-first day of the seventh month that Haggai gave his second message to the people. This was the last day of the Feast of Tabernacles. It was a special day. It was a day when everyone would be listening for the voice of God. To these disillusioned, discouraged, disspirited builders Haggai spoke on this feast day. He gave this message to the people: **'"Be strong...and work. For I am with you,'** says the Lord Almighty' (2:4).

Years later the Lord Jesus Christ gave a message. 'On the last and greatest day of the Feast, Jesus stood and said in a loud voice, "If anyone is thirsty, let him come to me and drink. Whoever believes in me, as the Scripture has said, streams of living water shall flow from within him' (John 7:37-38). Jesus spoke these words in the same temple which Zerubbabel was rebuilding. And it was on this same feast day that Jesus 'stood' and 'spoke'. In a loud voice he addressed needy souls. In Haggai's day the Jews were experiencing a literal drought of water, but Jesus came to quench a spiritual thirst. In Haggai's day the Jews were offered words of encouragement, but Jesus offered the people living water to quench their spiritual thirst.

'Be strong' and 'work'

Haggai urged the Jews to press on with the work. They were to **'be strong'** and **'work'**. Zerubbabel, Joshua and all the people were encouraged to 'be strong' (2:4). Some of the very old people among them would have seen the glorious splendour of Solomon's temple before the exile, and their own disillusionment with their present paltry efforts must have spread throughout the people from the rulers down to the ordinary citizens (2:3). In answer to their 'pouring of cold water' upon their present efforts, God sent Haggai to encourage them all to 'be strong' and 'work'.

This was the same call that had been given many years before to the high priest's namesake, Joshua. In Joshua 1:6-9 we read that God spoke to Moses' successor and said, 'Be strong and courageous, because you will lead these people to inherit the land...Be strong and very courageous. Be careful to obey all the law my servant Moses gave you...Have I not commanded you? Be strong and courageous. Do not be terrified; do not be discouraged, for the Lord your God will be with you wherever you go!'

Notice that there is a threefold call to be strong, both in the message to Joshua and here in these verses in Haggai. The promise of God's presence was likewise impressed on the hearers in both cases. They were to work despite their discouragements. They were to leave God to deal with the dangers and difficulties. Their task was to get on and rebuild the temple.

The same call was given by David to Solomon years before when he built the first temple. 'David also said to Solomon his son, "Be strong and courageous, and do the work. Do not be afraid or discouraged, for the Lord God, my God, is with you. He will not fail you or forsake you until all the work for the service of the temple of the Lord is finished"' (1 Chronicles 28:20).

Just as David told Solomon to act with determination in completing the first temple, so now the Lord uses the same language to stir the people to carry out their work of rebuilding. The task may be harder now, but the same God will supply the power.

A reminder of God's covenant

God had made a promise, a covenant with his people when they came out of Egypt: 'You yourselves have seen what I did to Egypt, and how I carried you on eagles' wings and brought you to myself. Now if you will obey me fully and keep my covenant, then out of all nations you will be my treasured possession. Although the whole earth is mine, you will be for me a kingdom of priests and a holy nation' (Exodus 19:4-6). God had kept his side of the arrangement. The people should do their part (i.e. be obedient to their God in everything that he commanded them). Haggai reminds them all of this when he said, **'This is what I covenanted with you when you came out of Egypt'** (2:5).

A promise of the presence of God's Spirit

'My Spirit remains among you. Do not fear' (2:5). Among other aspects of his name, the Holy Spirit is the power of God demonstrated. The Holy Spirit had been with Joshua, Saul and David. The same Holy Spirit had delivered the children of Israel from their Egyptian captors and brought them through the Red Sea. The Holy Spirit of God would also empower these Jewish builders under Zerubbabel and Joshua, the high priest. Notice the wording: the Holy Spirit does not come and go. He *remains* among them. In effect, Haggai is saying to them, 'God, the Spirit, is very much alive among you. He will stand his ground and lead you in this important work, so why be afraid?'

Money is no problem to God

Haggai tells them to have no anxious thoughts about where the money for the temple is coming from. 'That is no stumbling-block to building up the temple of the Lord. Listen to what the Lord says: **"The silver is mine and the gold is mine"'** (2:8). God made the minerals in the earth; they are his! He will provide from his own bounty all that is necessary for this glorious work. Haggai speaks to these worried builders and says, 'Don't worry that you won't be able to decorate the outside of the temple with beaten gold and ornamentations like Solomon's temple. God is more concerned about the desires of your hearts than the outward splendour of your work.'

So we see that, in the middle of their discouragement, Haggai encourages them.

God will provide the glory

'"I will fill this house with glory," says the Lord Almighty' (2:7). God says to these discouraged builders, 'You do your part and build the temple and I will come and fill it with my glory. I am with you and my Spirit is present in your midst. I am shortly going to work mightily.'

Encouragement for today

We should not be discouraged in the work of the gospel.
God's word holds good for us today: 'Be strong...and work.'
There are many things which can easily discourage us in the
work of the kingdom. The enormity of the task sometimes
overwhelms us and the enemy of souls seems so powerful.
The advance of the gospel seems so slow and the growth of the
church so meagre. Yet the same powerful Lord is with us as
was with Joshua and Zerubbabel. 'Let us not become weary
in doing good, for at the proper time we will reap a harvest if
we do not give up' (Galatians 6:9).

The disciples of Jesus were terrified when they were on the
Lake of Galilee and they saw Jesus walking towards them, so
he said to them, 'Take courage!' It is I. Don't be afraid' (Mark
6:50). We can be encouraged today when we remind ourselves that the presence of Christ can be just as real for us as it
was for the saints of bygone days. He has not altered. His
power has not diminished and he can still give us strength for
the work God has laid upon us. We must listen for his voice
and obey his command and the work will be done for his
glory.

Upheaval in the nations

Since the nuclear age has been with us people have often been
fearful of bringing children into a world where such dreadful
destruction could take place in a split second. The Jews of
Haggai's time were also anxious about the power of the
nations around them. 'They trembled before the consolidated
power of Persia, and the craft of Samaria that might bring that
power upon them again in restraint, if not in vengeance.'[2]
These things also made them hesitate to get on with the
rebuilding work. In the face of the powerful nations around
them the Lord Almighty says, 'In a little while I will once
more shake the heavens and the earth, the sea and the dry
land. I will shake all nations' (2:6:7).

God had done a fair bit of 'shaking' in the past. He humbled proud Egypt by the ten plagues (Exodus 7-12) and the destruction of Pharaoh's army in the Red Sea (Exodus 14:21-31). Psalm 68:7-8 describes these events as a 'shaking'. The Lord had shaken heaven and earth, sea and dry land when Babylon was overthrown in order to deliver Israel from exile (Isaiah 13:1-22; Jeremiah 50:46).[3]

God says he will do this again, and soon, **'in a little while'**. He says, 'I will come like an earthquake, unexpectedly and with great force.' The powers in Babylon will be shaken; its social and political base will be overthrown. God is saying, I am going to rearrange the nations. All you have to do, Judah, is to stand back and see my mighty actions.' Haggai said, 'Don't fear all those powerful nations. God has them in his hands. He is going to shake them for his own purposes, and that will all work out for your good.'

Many empires did fall during the next five centuries, the period up until the time of Christ. The Persian Empire, the Syrian Empire, Egypt and Babylon all fell before the empire of Greece. Then Greece in turn was crushed before the legions of mighty Rome. All these 'shakings' served God's purposes to prepare the way for the spread of the Messiah's kingdom.

How did these 'shakings' serve God's purposes? The Greek Empire helped greatly. Alexander's conquests served to spread Greek culture throughout the whole of the then known world. Greek became the universal language, instead of the many different tongues used previously. Most of the New Testament was written in Greek.

Then God used the Roman power for his purposes in taking the Christian message throughout the world. The Romans built marvellous roads which ran everywhere. (We still have some fine examples in Britain today of those long, straight highways.) These roads were good, quick and safe to travel upon. They helped to spread trade and the traders took the message of salvation to the furthest corners of the empire.

Also there was the *Pax Romana* (the Roman peace) which guaranteed safety and protection to citizens throughout the length and breadth of the empire.

God shook the nations to produce a common language for

the conveying of his gospel message. Easy travel and the stability of the Roman Empire also contributed to the spread of the Word.

The 'desired of all nations'

Who or what is 'the desired of all nations'? This is the most difficult part of this section. Many of us have been brought up with Charles Wesley's interpretation in the well-known Christmas hymn 'Hark the Herald Angels sing'.

> Come, Desire of nations, come,
> Fix in us thy humble home:
> Rise, the woman's conquering Seed,
> Bruise in us the serpent's head:
> Sing we then, with angels sing,
> 'Glory to the new-born King!
> Glory in the highest heaven,
> Peace on earth, and sins forgiven.'

This equates the 'desired of all nations' with the coming of the Messiah into the temple. God always refers to the temple as 'this house'. History talks of Solomon's temple, Zerubbabel's temple and Herod's temple, but in fact God only refers to one temple, 'this house'. Jesus entered this same temple on several occasions. He later taught there. The first time he was taken to 'this house' was as an eight-day-old baby for the rite of circumcision. Old Simeon took the child in his arms and praised God saying:

> 'Sovereign Lord, as you have promised,
>   You now dismiss your servant in peace.
> For my eyes have seen your salvation,
>   which you have prepared in the sight of all people,
> a light for revelation to the Gentiles
>   and for glory to your people Israel'
>
>   (Luke 2:29-32).

This was a fulfilment of Haggai's prophecy that **'The**

desired of all nations will come, and I will fill this house with glory.' What could be more glorious than the presence of the King of glory in his temple?

However, many scholars, ancient and modern, argue that the primary interpretation of this passage is not Messianic, although it has some reference to Christ. Moore says that this verse cannot refer to Christ: 'He is not the desire of all nations, but rather their aversion'[4] (see Isaiah 53:2). Calvin and others take the phrase to refer to the good things of the nations, all that was excellent among them, with especial reference to their wealth. Isaiah 60:5 says, 'The wealth on the seas will be brought to you, to you the riches of the nations will come.'

Haggai is, therefore, referring to Christ's kingdom. He is saying that God's chosen people, from every tribe and language, people and nation, will come and make up a great kingdom of priests to serve the Lord (Revelation 5:9). God will fill this house with glory. The glory of the Lord *and* his people will fill this house.

A bright future promised

'The glory of this present house will be greater than the glory of the former house' (2:9). Haggai is relaying God's encouragement to these disillusioned builders. He says, 'Don't worry about the outward looks. It is the heart that matters. Glory is more than gold-plated towers. Glory is the presence of the Lord Almighty in the midst of his redeemed, worshipping people.'

But the question must have still arisen in the minds of the builders: 'How can this latter temple be more glorious than Solomon's?' In Solomon's there were many things that were now missing. The ark and the other four 'marks of the temple' had been lost or destroyed when Nebuchadnezzar sacked the temple in 587 B.C. How could this temple be more glorious when it would not contain these religious articles?

'It will be more glorious,' said God, 'because it is the place where I will dwell and grant peace' (2:9). The Aaronic blessing of Numbers 6:24-26 had been known by the Jews for many centuries. It would be spoken again by the priest at the daily morning and evening sacrifice when the temple began functioning as the house of the Lord.

> 'The Lord bless you
>   and keep you;
> the Lord make his face shine upon you
>   and be gracious to you;
> the Lord turn his face towards you
>   and give you peace.'

'This peace is here guaranteed by the Lord of hosts, the Ruler of the Universe. While the Old Testament believers looked forward to the coming of the Prince of Peace, the New Testament points to the Cross of Calvary: It is finished! God was in Christ, reconciling the world unto himself' (2 Corinthians 5:19-20).[5] When Haggai said, **'I will grant peace,'** he meant it would be an ever-recurring granting of peace.

What is the New Testament temple?

The temple is none other than the blood-bought people of God. Listen to Paul: 'Don't you know that you yourselves are God's temple and that God's Spirit lives in you?' (1 Corinthians 3:16). 'Do you not know that your body is a temple of the Holy Spirit, who is in you?' (1 Corinthians 6:19) 'What agreement is there between the temple of God and idols? For we are the temple of the living God. As God has said: "I will live with them and walk among them, and I will be their God, and they will be my people"' (2 Corinthians 6:16).

The house of the Lord is the place where God is pleased to dwell and where he will grant peace to his people. Furthermore he will go on granting it. In Jesus, and only in him, can we know true and lasting peace: 'Peace I leave with you; my peace I give you. I do not give to you as the world gives. Do not let your hearts be troubled and do not be afraid' (John 14:27).

Differences between the Old and New Testament temples

The temple we are called upon to build is different in some ways from the material temple of the Old Testament.[6]

In the Old Testament God's temple was built of stone, wood and metal. These are all dead materials, however precious. God's temple in the New Testament is built of living stones, to become a dwelling in which God lives by his Spirit (Ephesians 2:19-22; 1 Peter 2:4-8).

In the Old Testament God's dwelling-place was confined to one nation, the people of Israel. In the New Covenant it includes members of every tribe and language and people and nation.

In the Old Testament God dwelt among his nation (believers and unbelievers alike). The glory of the New Testament temple, the church of God, is that it is a holy church: all of its members are washed, all are sanctified and all are justified in the name of the Lord Jesus Christ by the Spirit of God; it is a communion of saints.

The church of Jesus Christ is a church 'filled with glory' (Ephesians 5:25-27), which will reach its full perfection in the world to come as the church triumphant, without spot or wrinkle, holy and without blemish (Revelation 21:1-3).

6.
The weary builders

Message 3
18 December 520 B.C.

Please read Haggai 2:10-19

Exactly three months after the rebuilding of the temple commenced (see 1:14-15) Haggai again arrived on the scene with
a further message from the Lord. This message came **'to'**
Haggai, not 'through' as in 1:1 and 2:1. Perhaps this was to
indicate that it was directed to a more restricted audience
than the whole company of the returned exiles. In 2:20 the
message also came 'to' Haggai. On that occasion it was aimed
at only one man, Zerubbabel, and here, in 2:10-19, it is
initially the priests who are singled out for attention.

Let us consider what was happening. For two months the
Jews had been working steadily on the rebuilding of the
temple. They had sunk their feelings about the comparative
shabbiness of this restored building and were now plodding
on with the work. They were obeying the Lord's command to
'build the house' (1:8) but, it seems, they were not doing it
with whole-hearted energy and enthusiasm. Between Haggai's second message (2:1-9) and his third message (2:10-19)
another prophet began to speak God's Word in Jerusalem.
Zechariah started to prophesy to these same people in the
eighth month of the second year of Darius (Zechariah 1:1).
That was in the month commencing on 27 October, by our
calendar.

Zechariah was sent by God to call the people to repentance. He reminded them of the stubbornness of their
forefathers in refusing to return to the ways of the Lord. He
said: 'The Lord was very angry with your forefathers. Therefore tell the people: This is what the Lord Almighty says:
"Return to me," declares the Lord Almighty, "and I will
return to you," says the Lord Almighty. Do not be like your

forefathers, to whom the earlier prophets proclaimed: This is what the Lord Almighty says: "Turn from your evil ways and your evil practices." But they would not listen or pay attention to me, declares the Lord. Where are your forefathers now? And the prophets, do they live for ever? But did not my words and my decrees, which I commanded my servants the prophets, overtake your forefathers?' Then they repented and said, "The Lord Almighty has done to us what our ways and our practices deserve, just as he determined to do"'(Zechariah 1:2-6).

The people had been working, and had not given up. Outwardly everything seemed fine, but their hearts were not right. They had grown very lethargic in their efforts to build up the temple. They had become weary in their work for the Lord, and so far, they had refused to see anything wrong in their half-hearted attitude.

The attitude of the builders

Haggai had mixed among the people and he had noticed that their heart was not in the work. He perceived how they were thinking: 'This is just one more task which has to be done, so we might as well get it over with as soon as possible. Then we can have a rest.' How was Haggai going to encourage the builders to be more zealous? He looked upwards. He did not take his orders, nor get his ideas from men. He was in touch with the Lord Almighty. He knew that God was in charge of the situation. He realized that the Lord knew the best way to get the people to work willingly and with the right spirit, so he passed on the word which God had given to him. He used a well-tried teaching method to get his message across. He referred to something they knew about and then moved them, in their thinking, to something which was new to them.

Haggai consulted the priests

The priests were the experts in the law. They were the authorized expounders of the *Torah* (Leviticus 10:11; Ezekiel 44:23). Their ruling was accepted as authoritative. The people looked up to them because they were the spiritual leaders among the Jews. They taught the law and they were responsible for preparing and offering sacrifices upon the altar of the Lord.

Haggai asked the priests two questions.

1. He spoke about consecrated meat (2:12)

This was meat which had been sanctified. (It had been set apart for a special reason.) It had been prepared for offering to the Lord and it had been carried in the usual way, in the folds of the priests' garments. This was a common sight. Everyone knew that, automatically, the cloth which was wrapped around the sacrifice would be made holy too, because it carried the sacrificial meat (see Leviticus 6:27). 'Now' asked Haggai, 'what happens if that cloth touches some ordinary food? Is that food sanctified too?' 'Of course not,' was the emphatic answer from the priests. 'Their reply was correct, for although the garment was made holy by the offering it contained, it had no power to transmit that sacredness any further.'[1]

2. Haggai asks about the contamination of holy things (2:13).

His argument went on like this: 'All right, then, this ordinary food can't be made holy by coming into contact with something which contains sanctified meat, but what about if this same ordinary food is touched by someone who has been in contact with a dead body (which the Jews considered unclean)? Does this person render the food unclean?' Notice that there is no direct contact between the dead body and the ordinary food. This time the answer is different. The priests said, 'Yes. The ordinary food has become defiled because of the intermediary' (see Leviticus 11:28; 22:4-7).

Haggai applied this teaching to the people

Having established the scriptural principles, Haggai then said, **'So it is with this people and this nation in my sight,'**

declares the Lord. 'Whatever they do and whatever they offer there is defiled' (2:14).

Notice that it is the Lord who is making this solemn declaration. He is consistent with the teaching of his own Word. (This is a very vital principle for any prophecy.) And he says that the actions of the people are being done 'in my sight'. Remember that 'Man looks at the outward appearance, but the Lord looks at the heart' (1 Samuel 16:7). God could see into their inmost beings and he observed their half-heartedness in the task of rebuilding.

Again God refers to the Jews as 'this people' and 'this nation'. He had previously called them 'this people' in 1:2 while they were being disobedient. Now they are again disobeying him and disobedience causes a barrier between God and the people.

Why was there a barrier between God and the people? It came about because the people, who were offering sacrifices upon the altar, were contaminated: 'Whatever they offer there [i.e. upon the altar] is defiled.' The people assumed that because they were offering sacrifices to God upon the altar, (which had been used for many years) this outward action would make them holy and secure the protection and blessing of God for them. They assumed that because they were working on a holy building they would automatically become holy themselves; but they were defiled, said the Lord (2:14).

Why were the people unclean? Their lethargic attitude had made, them unclean. Their love, their loyalty, their enthusiasm for God's work had all begun to diminish. They thought that their good work in offering sacrifices upon the altar would make up for their lack of zeal for God's house. They thought their devout actions would make them acceptable in God's eyes. They believed they were pleasing God by offering sacrifices to him. But the psalmist said of the Lord,

> 'You do not delight in sacrifice, or I would bring it;
>   you do not take pleasure in burnt offerings.
> The sacrifices of God are a broken spirit;
>   a broken and contrite heart,
>   O God, you will not despise'
>
> (Psalm 51:16-17).

What did God think of the Jews' attitude to the rebuilding work? God was saying, in effect, 'It is no use. The builders of my house must have pure hearts.' What God was saying through Haggai was this: 'You can't catch holiness. It is God's gift to those who commit themselves completely to him and his service.' A cold can be caught (just as defilement can be caught from a dead body) but health is different. It cannot be caught (any more than a sanctified garment can transfer its holiness to anyone who touches it).

Sin is extremely contagious. It only takes one small drop of poison to contaminate a whole glass of water, but even a large amount of wholesome water will not purify a bowl which contains an impurity. We need to recognize that our lives are tainted with sin which, like physical illness, is all too contagious. Our good works will not atone for our sinfulness. Only repentance and faith in Christ will save us.

God demands pure actions, attitudes and motives from his workers. God will never accept unworthy sacrifices. Those who are engaged in building up the church of Jesus Christ must seek to have 'clean hands'. Those who minister in the house of the Lord should endeavour to come before God's people with a wholesome spirit. If people try to offer praise and worship to God in their own strength and with mixed motives (e.g. so that they will receive the praise of men) the Lord will not be pleased to receive such worship.

The only sacrifice which is acceptable to God is that which was offered by his own precious Son on the cross at Calvary. Only as we are 'alive in him' will our offerings of praise and worship be acceptable in God's sight.

Some serious thinking

As a result of Haggai's appeal, the priests and all the people were compelled to think hard. God said, **"Now give careful thought to this from this day on"** (2:15). The phrase 'from this day on' (literally 'upward') is a Hebrew idiom which was 'capable of reference backwards as well as forwards in time. Like a signpost it stood at the parting of the ways, pointing back over the road already travelled and on to the way ahead.'[2] The footnote in the NIV gives 'to the days past', and also notice that verse 15 continues, **'consider how things were before...'**

'Consider' is not a harsh word, as it is used here, in 1:5 and 7. The emphasis here and in 2:18 is to encourage. Haggai tells the people to think about what happened before they started building (2:15-16). He reminds them that when they came to assess the quantity of grain in a heap of corn stacks they thought, from the look of it, that they would get twenty measures of wheat out of it. Yet when it came to be threshed, it only produced ten. It was even worse when it came to the produce of the vineyard. They thought that they would end up with fifty measures of wine in the storage vat, but when the grapes were trodden, all they got were twenty – less than half what they were expecting.

Why was there such a poor harvest? 'I caused it,' said the Lord. **'I struck all the work of your hands with blight, mildew and hail, yet you did not turn to me,' declares the Lord** (2:17). This was the curse that God had told the Israelites he would send on them if they disobeyed his commands (Deuteronomy 28:22). This is virtually the same as the message given by Amos:

> '"Many times I struck your gardens and vineyards,
>   I struck them with blight and mildew.
> Locusts devoured your fig and olive trees,
>   yet you have not returned to me,'
>
> > declares the Lord"
> > (Amos 4:9).

In 1:9 God had said, 'You expected a good harvest, but you reaped little. And even the little you gathered produced far, far less than you expected when it was processed.' Now he is saying the same thing again. 'Give careful thought to what is happening around you. It is caused by your disobedience. I sent it to encourage you to repent, to turn to me.'

What were the people doing? These people were building the temple of the Lord. In 2:15 and 18 a different word for temple is used. 'Up to this point, *house* has been the standard designation, but now a word which can also mean "palace" is used. Haggai may be stressing God's position as King of the universe, one whose house should indeed be a palace.'[3]

The people were working on God's temple, yet they had defiled hands. The message here is that those who are half-hearted in their efforts to build God's palace are not worthy to be engaged in such a sacred task. Those who are dis-obedient to God's clear commands have no right to be work-ing on God's temple. David asks,

> 'Who may ascend the hill of the Lord?
>   Who may stand in his holy place?
> He who has clean hands and a pure heart,
>   who does not lift up his soul to an idol
>   or swear by what is false.
> *He* will receive the blessing from the Lord
>   and vindication from God his Saviour'

(Psalm 24:3-5).

A new attitude

What happened when they were called upon to think about their crops? Following this call there seems to have been genuine repentance among the people. God calls them to think carefully about what they are doing. He reminds them of their rebuilding work. He refers to the laying of the foun-dations of the Lord's temple (2:18). (This happened way back in 536 B.C., see Ezra 3:10.) He talks about 'one stone being laid upon another' (2:15). And he says, 'Think carefully about this' twice in 2:18.

At last they appear to be listening to God. There seems to be a new attitude among them. They can no longer ignore what the Lord is saying to them by these natural disasters which have befallen them, and they realize that if only they would return to the Lord whole-heartedly something wonder-ful would happen.

God asked them about their reserves of food. **'Is there yet any seed left in the barn?'** (2:19). The answer is 'No. We have had to sow every grain in the field with the hope that there will be a better harvest next spring.' As the people thought about the implication of their situation, they realized that they could do nothing more about the harvest. The fields had been ploughed. The seed had been sown. Now all they could do was wait, hope and pray, until there were signs of growth appearing in the fields.

It is as though the Lord were saying to them, 'Now what's going to happen? Think how you have fared in recent years with figs, pomegranates and olives (2:19). They haven't borne fruit, yet you did the right thing. You did it at the right time and in the proper way, but despite all of that, you only got a very small return for your efforts.'

Great news!

'Listen carefully to me,' says the Lord. 'This winter's day is going to be the beginning of something great. You are half expecting to continue to plod on as you have been up until now, but listen,' says the Lord, *'I am going to do a new thing!'* 'From this eighteenth day of December, and onwards, I will bless you' (2:19). Despite your slowness, despite your lack of faith, despite your weariness in the work, despite your stubbornness to trust me, despite your half-heartedness, I, the Lord Almighty am going to bless you abundantly. At the moment you can't see what is happening. You can't see the seed in the soil; but it is beginning to sprout. Are you thinking it will be another meagre harvest? Well, you are wrong. There will be an abundant ingathering of produce.'

Haggai is so sure of God's word that he 'sticks his neck out' and says, **'From this day on,'** says God, **'I will bless you.'** 'This is a promise wholly unmerited.' The people for a long period of years absolutely refused to obey God's command to build the temple, and even now they were not too willing to carry on. And yet the God of infinite grace and mercy (Exodus 34:6) is ready to pour out his blessings on them. Who, indeed, is a God like unto the Lord? (Micah 7:18-19).[4]

Sowing the seed

The figure changes during this third message from a building (the temple) to a field. These are both scriptural ways of describing the work of preaching the gospel and gathering converts into the church of Jesus Christ. When we do the work of evangelism (sowing the precious seed) we do not know what is going on in people's minds (below the surface of the ground). We cannot judge the effectiveness of our witnessing by outward visible signs. Whatever appears to be happening or not happening, we are called to preach the Word, whether in season or out of season (2 Timothy 4:2). Even when there is no apparent indication of spiritual blessing we should rejoice in the goodness of God because whether or not we see signs of success, God is at work.

> 'Though the fig-tree does not bud
>   and there are no grapes on the vines,
> though the olive crop fails
>   and the fields produce no food,
> though there are no sheep in the pen
>   and no cattle in the stalls,
> yet I will rejoice in the Lord,
> I will be joyful in God my Saviour'
>
> (Habbakuk 3:17-18).

The signs of blessing began to show when the foundation of the Lord's temple was laid, when his people became obedient to his Word. Today God is building his people into his church. He is placing one stone upon another and they are fitting together and growing into a spiritual house for his glory (Ephesians 2:19-22), and he will fill his church with the glory and grandeur of his presence. God's blessing will come. Let us trust him and eagerly look forward to that time of great spiritual prosperity when he will gather thousands and thousands into his church. Revival will come.

There may be nothing left in the barn. We may not have anything that we can fall back on; all our resources may be committed to the work of God, yet God says, 'From this day on I will bless you.' God is saying to his obedient people today, 'You, unworthy builders of my temple, you weary Sunday School teachers, you inadequate preachers of the gospel, you timid witnesses of mine, from this day onwards, because you have repented of your iniquity and your lethargy and have obeyed my commands, I will bless you and make your efforts glorious in my sight.'

And the blessing will be so great that the people who care nothing for the things of God will walk by and say, 'Whatever is happening?' and God's people will reply, 'Come and see what God is doing among his people in these days of great blessing.'

7.
The chosen builder

Message 4
18 December 520 B.C.

Please read Haggai 2:20-23

Dreadful things are going on in the world today, enough to make any thoughtful person tremble and fear. At any time some crazy person in Moscow or Washington could press that button and cause a great nuclear catastrophe to engulf the whole world. We could all be wiped out in a second, and those left behind would have an existence not worth living. If we really thought about these things, we would go insane and be plagued with continual nightmares.

The Jews were worried by the international scene

'The Jews were surrounded on all sides by inveterate enemies, they had as many enemies as they had neighbours; and they were hated even by the whole world.'[1] They were still under Persian authority and there was tremendous upheaval going on in Babylon. The ruling authorities were starting to be challenged and when that happened it was certain that someone's head would roll. It is very frightening when great nations become involved in strife, especially when there is a lack of firm leadership, and brother seeks to stab brother in the back (2:22). Selfishness is all that matters then. In that situation you can be sure that the affairs of small nations will count for nothing. Government officials will be more concerned for their own prestige than the welfare of others.

What happened in Babylon would be bound to affect Judah. But who cared about the Jews? They were a very small nation, unimportant in global terms. They were not worth worrying about. No wonder the inhabitants of Judah trembled when they considered what was likely to erupt around them. Was there any point in doing anything other than looking after their own skins?

What about the temple? Imagine the conversations taking place at that time. 'Is there any use in continuing to build God's house? It's pretty shabby anyway. No self-respecting God will want to dwell in this building. Is it worthwhile even carrying on with our religion? What will the end of it all be? Does anyone care what will happen to us?'

God shows his hand

But God did care, and he showed his hand yet again. God had already spoken once that day, through his servant Haggai (2:10-19). He had warned the people about their half-hearted work for him. He had urged them to consider carefully how they were behaving, and he had promised, against all odds, that there would be great blessing from that very day forwards, that is from 18 December 520 B.C. (2:19). Now God speaks again on this same twenty-fourth day of the ninth month of the second year of King Darius.

You will have noticed that, for the first time, Haggai gives his message to just one person, Zerubbabel. Joshua the high priest is not included, nor are the remnant of the people. It is Zerubbabel who is chosen for special mention in the concluding verses of this prophecy.

Why was Zerubbabel singled out?

After all, it was Joshua who would be crowned. Zechariah said, 'The word of the Lord came to me... "Take the silver and gold and make a crown, and set it on the head of the high priest, Joshua son of Jehozadak. Tell him this is what the Lord Almighty says: 'Here is the man whose name is the Branch, and he will branch out from his place and build the temple of the Lord. It is he who will build the temple of the

Lord, and he will be clothed with majesty and will sit and rule on his throne. And he will be a priest on his throne'"" (Zechariah 6:9-13).

Why had Zerubbabel been passed over for kingship? The answer is that he has not been ignored. Joshua is to be crowned a *priest* (Zechariah 6:13), but here in Haggai 2:21-23 great promises are made to Zerubbabel. God addresses him directly. He is to be a mighty champion of the people in their time of great need. Zerubbabel is chosen as God's leader of the people.

In this last message God does not address him as Zerubbabel the ruler, (he had called him by the title 'governor' in 1:1,14; 2:2,21). Now he gives him another designation. Zerubbabel is called God's 'servant'. 'There can be no higher title in the Bible.'[2] Moses was called by God 'my servant' (Numbers 12:7); so was David (Ezekiel 34:23) and Daniel was called the 'servant of the living God' (Daniel 6:20). In Isaiah chapters 52 and 53 we have the so-called 'servant songs' and in Luke 22:27 we read that Jesus said to his disciples, 'I am among you as one who serves.' Now Zerubbabel will have this honour of serving God among the Jews. He will receive his orders from the Lord. He will be obedient to God and he will carry out the clear commands given by his almighty Lord.

Zerubbabel is to be like God's signet ring

A signet ring was very important to ancient kings. It was the representation of its owner. It was used for sealing official documents and was worn either on the finger, like a ring (Jeremiah 22:24), or on a chain around the neck in the form of a cylinder with a raised impression upon it (Genesis 38:18).

A signet ring was very precious. It was never to leave the body of the person to whom it was entrusted. Usually the king or ruler wore it himself. God was saying to Zerubbabel, 'I have chosen you to keep safely this sign of my decrees.' The governor was to be like God's signet ring because he was to ensure that God's commands would be clearly given. His seal would verify as authentic the declaration of God. What a great honour was given to Zerubbabel! He was to be like

God's signet ring. He was to have the privilege and responsibility of issuing God's orders to the people.

Why was Zerubbabel so honoured? It was certainly not because he had earned the distinction, for he had to be cajoled into resuming the work on the temple. Many of us would have felt that a few months before he was a total failure and not worthy of any spiritual responsibilities. He, like everyone else, was not blessed by God because of any merit or good works of his own; he was given this exalted position because God stated, 'I have chosen you.' Zerubbabel had been called out from among the people. He had been raised up for this purpose. He was God's chosen servant and his signet ring was his authority to be as a divinely appointed king among the people. 'This petty prince of Judah (Ezra 1:8), a small impoverished nation under foreign dominion, was honoured by the supreme ruler of the world and his church, the Lord of hosts, to be a prominent link in that illustrious chain of ancestors (Matthew 1:1,6,12 and Luke 3:23,27), extending from King David to Jesus Christ, the God-man, King of kings and Lord of lords.'[3]

'God is still on the throne'

In this last message in Haggai God is telling Zerubbabel not to fear. God is going to deal with the situation. 'Don't worry about the political upheaval going on around you, Zerubbabel. Don't be over-anxious about your little Jewish country. Don't fear what will happen; because I am at work.'

This was God's message to Zerubbabel: 'There will be great shakings, overturnings, overthrowings and fallings. These nations are very powerful but I am more powerful still. **I will shake the heavens and the earth. I will overturn royal thrones and shatter the power of foreign kingdoms. I will overthrow chariots and their drivers; horses and their riders will fall'** (2:21-22).

God amplified the message about 'shaking' that he had spoken through Haggai in 2:6. He said that the terrible upheaval of the nations will largely come from within themselves. 'This fighting among themselves characterized the response of the

Midianites to Gideon's surprise attack in Judges 7:22, and
there are two eschatological passages which employ the same
idiom (in Ezekiel 38:19-23 and Zechariah 14:13-14).'[4] All this
havoc will be caused by the Lord God Almighty. Notice the
three-times repeated, **'I will'** in verses 21 and 23. Also see
how violent the verbs are. Just as God *hurled* Pharaoh's
chariots and his army into the sea (Exodus 15:4), so this same
God will appear on behalf of the Jews and cause their enemies
to be *cast down*. God said, 'Do not fear. I am with you. I will
protect you. I will keep you. I have chosen you, Zerubbabel,
for my royal purposes.' Stuart Olyott sums it up like this:
'God threw down kingdoms and elevated a particular individual to a place of honour.'[5]

What happened to Zerubbabel?

Did he reign as a king of Judah? No. He is reckoned to have
been at the dedication of the rebuilt temple four years later in
516 B.C. (Ezra 6:14-15; Zechariah 4:9), but then he recedes
into the darkness of history. Why is this? Did God's promise
to him come to nothing? No. Zerubbabel was one of those
who 'were still living by faith when they died. They did not
receive the things promised: they only saw them and wel-
comed them from a distance' (Hebrews 11:13). What happened was that Zerubbabel (grandson of the last King of
Judah) became part of that line of descent which led to the
coming of the great Messiah of God's people. He is mentioned in both Matthew 1:12-13 and in Luke 3:27 as being an
ancestor (by the flesh) of Jesus Christ.

Zerubbabel was an obedient forerunner of our blessed
Lord. He got on with the work God gave him to do of rebuilding the temple. He did it faithfully, loyally and cheerfully, and
God honoured him for his labours in the house of the Lord.
'Later generations thought very highly of Zerubbabel. His
name is included with that of Joshua among the famous men
of the fathers of Israel (Ecclesiasticus 49:11), and even today
it occurs in the *Hanukkah* hymn recounting God's deliver-
ances: "Well nigh had I perished, when Babylon's end drew
near; through Zerubbabel I was saved after seventy years."'[6]

God is with his people today

Jesus said, 'You will hear of wars and rumours of wars, but see to it that you are not alarmed. Such things must happen, but the end is still to come. Nation will rise against nation, and kingdom against kingdom. There will be famines and earthquakes in various places' (Matthew 24:6-7). 'I am with you; do not fear,' is still the word of the Lord for his people. 'God predicts that thrones will fall, along with their military capacity. Chariots and horses represent the epitome of strength for ancient warfare. Significantly, the word *power* or *strength* occurs in the verbal form rendered "take courage" in 2:4. If the Lord is the strength of our lives, our security surpasses that of the most powerful nations with all their weapons.'[7]

God's people will be like the mysterious bush at Horeb. They will live on unconsumed and unconsumable in the midst of destroying armies. They are guarded by the eternal purposes of God. Calvin says, 'God still shakes [the heaven and the earth] today, when the gospel is preached; for he forms anew the children of Adam after his image. This spiritual regeneration is such an evidence of God's power and grace, that he may justly be said to shake the heaven and the earth.'[8]

God's seal is on his people

When we believe in the Lord Jesus Christ and receive him as our own personal Saviour, he seals us. 'He anointed us, set his seal of ownership on us, and put his Spirit in our hearts as a deposit, guaranteeing what is to come' (2 Corinthians 1:22).

In New Testament times a merchant would go to market and buy a pile of grain. Into the side of this heap he would press a stamp bearing his own special mark of ownership. Later his servant would come along and look for a stack of grain bearing his master's symbol. When he found it, with the mark still intact, he would know that no one had attempted to remove any of the corn because the pattern was a perfect impression of his master's seal. So in Ephesians 1:13-14 we read, 'And you also were included in Christ when you heard the word of truth, the gospel of your salvation. Having believed, you were marked in him with a seal, the promised Holy Spirit, who is a deposit guaranteeing our inheritance until the redemption of those who are God's possession – to the praise of his glory.'

We too are builders

In the lovely picture of the vine and the branches Jesus said of his people, 'You did not choose me, but I chose you' (John 15:16). Why did he choose us? He chose us 'to go and bear fruit – fruit that will last'. When we became Christians it is not merely because of our decision to follow Jesus, it is because God has called us. We are referred to as 'those who have been called' (Romans 8:28). John says that 'We love because he first loved us' (1 John 4:19). Indeed, 'He chose us in [Christ] before the creation of the world to be holy and blameless in his sight' (Ephesians 1:4)

As Zerubbabel was chosen for the purpose of building the temple, so one of the purposes of God's people is to edify God's building, that is, his people (Romans 14:19). God has called us to be builders of his church. It is largely in ruins now and it is our duty to heed his call to 'build the house' (1:8). The church is God's appointed means of gospel witness. He designed that his people should be in fellowship with others. He has called us not just to be a 'holy huddle' but to get on with the task of building for his glory.

'A happy church is one that is giving and going , one that is reaching out, that does not have time to think how it feels today, because it is in the business of sharing the life of Jesus with the world in which Christ has placed it... You do not go to church on Sunday mornings only in order to have a good time together with other Christians. You go in order to penetrate your world during the week, more effectively for Christ.'[9]

8.
Today's builders

Haggai lived a long time ago. The building he was responsible for was later beautified by the hated Herod and finally destroyed by the Romans in A.D. 70 (except for a few foundation stones in the west wall). What relevance does Haggai's call have to us, when he tells us that the Lord God Almighty says, 'Go up to the hills and bring wood and build the house, that I may take pleasure in it and that I may appear in my glory'? (Haggai 1:8 RSV).

The church of Jesus Christ is sometimes described as a building (1 Corinthians 3:9-10; Ephesians 2:21; 1 Peter 2:5), but nowhere in the New Testament do we read of a local church erecting a building of bricks and mortar for the purpose of worship. The early Christians met for worship in the temple and then went to each other's homes for fellowship (Acts 2:46). I have a friend who maintains that it is quite wrong for churches to meet anywhere other than in people's homes; even the hiring of a hall must be for a limited time and a specific purpose (as Paul hired the hall of Tyrannus in Acts 19:9-10). Why, then, do we often read about the need to build up the church, and why did Jesus say, 'I will build my church'? (Matthew 16:18).

Each time the figure of a building is used to describe the called-out people of God it is to paint a picture of a growing structure. The church is not yet complete. A concordance gives many verses which show the need for God's people to be engaged in building up one another in the faith. Romans 14:19 says, 'Let us ... make every effort to do what leads to peace and to mutual edification.' In Ephesians 4 Paul speaks about God's gift of his servants, 'so that the body of Christ may be built up' (v.12). He says the body is growing 'and builds itself up in love' (v.16). He also encourages the right use of the tongue 'for building others up according to their needs' (v.29).

The similarities between Haggai's days and our day

Just as the ruined temple was a disgrace in the days when Haggai started to preach, so the church today shows great signs of decay. If we are to obey God's commands and 'build the house' much needs to be done. Leading theologians are denying the fundamentals of the faith. Men are using the church today to preach their political and sociological ideas, while all around men, women and children are suffering and dying without the comfort and solace that the gospel of the Lord Jesus Christ alone can bring them.

The church lies largely in ruins, and we will not escape judgement for our failure to be the temple of the living God. God is calling his people to become active and build his house, the church, for his glory.

Why are we to build the house?

We are to build it solely for God's glory. That means we are not to build it for man's glory. If we achieve anything at all, it is only because of God's grace. There is nothing of which we can boast. This is where the big mistake has often been made. We try to live as though we were meant to be in a man-centred environment. How foolish this is! There will be no future for any of us until God is at the centre of things. Man is nothing. We can only be anything of any value as we surrender ourselves to God and honestly desire to obey his commands. Jesus tells us the way to live is to 'deny ourselves, take up our cross and follow him' (Matthew 16:24).

How then can we build for God's glory? First of all we must be those who are truly seeking to honour him. We so often want to do what pleases us, but it is the honour of God that should always be our aim.

Does God have first place in your life? Is his will what truly counts in your life and in the life of your church? If we are not building a church for God's glory, we are wasting our time. 'Unless the Lord builds the house, its builders labour in vain' (Psalm 127:1).

Secondly, we honour God when the church grows. The house of the Lord is not being built unless there are true conversions, real trophies of grace, as they used to be called. We all need to look around our church fellowships and see how many believers there are today who a few months ago were heedless and careless of their eternal destiny. There also needs to be a restoration of backsliders and a great building up of the saints in their most holy faith.

So many churches are growing just because more people are being attracted to the fellowship by the performance of the preacher, the excitement of the worship, or the wide variety of activities going on in the week. Only as God is building up his church and adding to it will there be any real and lasting blessing. Man's building will not withstand the attacks of the Evil One. Paul said, 'If any man builds on this foundation using gold, silver, costly stones, wood, hay or straw, his work will be shown for what it is, because the Day will bring it to light. It will be revealed with fire, and the fire will test the quality of each man's work' (1 Corinthians 3:12-13).

How are we to build?

First of all we must start with the correct foundation. Paul speaks about this in 1 Corinthians 3:10-11: 'By the grace God has given me, I laid a foundation as an expert builder, and someone else is building on it. But each one should be careful how he builds. For no one can lay any foundation other than the one already laid, which is Jesus Christ.'

Then we are to see that the correct building materials are used in its erection. The house of God will not be built without a great deal of earnest prayer. John Blanchard has said, 'To attempt to work for God without prayer is as futile as trying to launch a space probe with a peashooter.' And Robert Haldane, the great Scottish reformer said, 'To pray without labouring is to mock God; to labour without prayer is to rob God of his glory.'[1]

The study of God's Word is another ingredient in building for God's glory. Unless people submit themselves to the teaching contained in the Bible they will build in their own strength and on shifting sand. A wise builder builds upon the rock (Matthew 7:24-27), for it is only Christ who is dependable and it is only the Word of God which speaks God's word to us. Those who say they can throw away their Bibles because they now have the Spirit of God are, to say the least, very foolish. Only in the Word of God do we discover God's truth, and only as the Holy Spirit applies that Word to our lives will we learn and be strengthened to go and build for God's glory.

Building is team-work. Where there is disagreement among the workers the structure being built will suffer. We should have a sincere love for our fellow Christians and 'love one another deeply, from the heart' (1 Peter 1:22). The secret of growth is to have a great love for Jesus Christ and for each other. We should be prepared to open up our hearts and our minds to one another. Do we not all need to be built up in this respect? A growing church is one that is increasing in the sense of fellowship which is being experienced among its members.

Humility is sometimes lacking among God's builders. We cannot expect to build the house for God's glory unless we 'in humility consider others better than [ourselves]' (Philippians 2:3). We are exhorted 'to walk humbly with [our] God' (Micah 6:8). We must come to see that, if anything is to be achieved of lasting value, it must be God's doing, not ours. We need more tears, more esteeming of others as greater than ourselves and more looking upward to God.

Who is to build?

We are. All those who belong to the Lord are being called upon to be energetic and active in this great work of building up what Jesus called 'my church'. Jesus Christ wants his house to be beautiful, glorious and powerful, for the glory of God. 'Christ loved the church and gave himself up for her to make her holy, cleansing her by the washing with water through the word' (Ephesians 5:25-26).

The Lord is in control

Have you noticed that the last three words in the prophecy of
Haggai are 'the Lord Almighty'? (Haggai 2:23). This reminds
us that the sovereign Lord of the Universe is in control. Whatever dangers and difficulties the people of God may have in
their labours for his glory, 'God is still on the throne', and we
must remember that we are building day by day for his, and
his glory alone, and the Lord Almighty is with us.

Zechariah

9.
Introduction to Zechariah

Please read Zechariah 1:1

Twenty-eight people are named Zechariah in the Old Testament. The word Zechariah means 'the Lord remembers' and this is the theme of the eleventh of the twelve 'minor' prophets. God remembers his covenant and his holy laws, which he expects his people to obey. He will be satisfied with nothing less than whole-hearted obedience to his commands. Yet he also remembers his promises and always keeps his word never to forsake his chosen people.

The prophecy of Zechariah has been called 'the Apocalypse of the Old Testament', because much of the book is similar in style and content to Revelation, the last book in the New Testament. As with Revelation, Zechariah is written to encourage the people of God in their work and witness. Times were tough for the first recipients of both books. In Zechariah's time the people needed to be encouraged to continue with the rebuilding of the temple, and to be enthusiastic for a life lived in obedience to God.

Two successful prophets

Zechariah was a contemporary of Haggai. Ezra 5:1 records that they both prophesied 'to the Jews in Judah in the name of the God of Israel, who was over them'. As a result of their preaching 'Zerubbabel son of Shealtiel and Jeshua son of Jozadak set to work to rebuild the house of God in Jerusalem,' but Haggai and Zechariah did not stand idly by. We observe that 'The prophets of God were with them, helping them' (Ezra 5:2). And when we read Ezra 6:14 we find

that the work is still going on: 'So the elders of the Jews continued to build and prosper under the preaching of Haggai the
prophet and Zechariah, a descendant of Iddo.'

These two prophets were faithful in their calling. They
urged the people to commence rebuilding the temple and
they encouraged them to continue with it. Although Haggai's
last recorded prophecy is on the twenty-fourth day of the
ninth month of the second year of King Darius, we note that
he is still with them at the completion of the temple on 'the
third day of the month Adar, in the sixth year of the reign of
King Darius' (Ezra 6:15). Unlike most of the prophets, both
Zechariah and Haggai lived to see the successful outcome of
their preaching.

So why do we have Zechariah as well as Haggai, if their task
was the same? If we study the dates carefully we see that their
ministries overlapped. Haggai started preaching two months
before Zechariah. As we saw in chapters 1-3, his first message, delivered on the first and twenty-fourth days of the sixth
month of the second year of King Darius, resulted in work
being resumed on the temple. Some weeks later, on the
twenty-first day of the seventh month, Haggai needed to give
a second message to encourage the builders; their efforts
were flagging when they saw that the rebuilt temple had little
of the glory of Solomon's temple. Haggai's final two messages
were not delivered until two months later (on the twenty-
fourth day of the ninth month). It was in between Haggai's
second and third messages that Zechariah began his
prophecy, some time in the eighth month of the second year
of King Darius.

While Haggai's short book and the first eight chapters of
Zechariah are both taken up with the need to rebuild the
house of the Lord at Jerusalem, the styles of these two
prophets differ. Dr J. Vernon MacGee says, 'Haggai was a
practical man. He carried a ruler with him. He said 2 + 2 = 4.
He measured the temple. Everything had to be brought right
down to the ground, laid out. He was not very romantic or
poetic, but he sure was practical. Zechariah was a dreamer.
Haggai had his feet on the ground. Zechariah had his head in
the clouds. Zechariah, for instance, saw a woman in a bushel
basket going through the air. Now friend, that's poetical.
Haggai'd never seen that ... You need the practical man and

the poet to walk along together and these were the two men God put together.'[1]

David Baron, in less colourful language, explains it like this: 'The difference between the two prophets seems to be this, that while Haggai's task was chiefly to rouse the people to the outward task of rebuilding the temple, Zechariah took up the prophetic labours just where Haggai had left it, and sought to lead the people to a complete spiritual change, one of the fruits of which would of necessity be increased zeal in the building of God's House, the completion of which he witnessed four years later.'[2]

The people were still very materialistic in their outlook. Their zeal was for ritual rather than for reliance on the Lord. Their concern was for respectability in religious observances rather than for an acknowledgement of their sin and a desire to please God in all their thoughts and actions. Their concern was for the erection of a smart building, rather than to be an expectant people waiting humbly on their God.

Who was Zechariah?

From the first verse of the prophecy we learn that his father's name was Berekiah and his grandfather was called Iddo. But in Ezra 5:1 there is no mention of Berekiah. Zechariah is simply called a descendant of Iddo. It would seem, then, that Berekiah had died before his own father, possibly while Zechariah was still quite young. This would explain why Zechariah is referred to as a descendant of Iddo.

In Nehemiah 12:16 we read that one of the heads of the priestly family was called Zechariah of the family of Iddo. It could well be that this Iddo and Zechariah are the same people referred to in Zechariah 1:1. It is likely, then, that the prophet Zechariah was also a priest. He certainly had intimate acquaintance with the temple, its rites and its equipment (see chapter 3: also 6:9-15; 9:8,15; 14:16,20-21).

Some scholars believe that the young man referred to in Zechariah 2:4 is Zechariah himself. If this is the case then he must have been not much older than a baby when he returned from the Babylonian captivity, and very young when he was called to the priesthood and the prophetic office.

The book of Zechariah

Zechariah's prophecy falls into two halves. Chapters 1-8 are
clearly dated and after a short introduction (1:1-6) we read of
eight visions concerning the rebuilding of the temple, Joshua
and Zerubbabel (the leaders of the people) and the spiritual
transformation of the people (chapters 1:7 – 6:15), followed
by some questions concerning fasting (7:1 – 8:23).

Chapters 9-14 are undated, and were probably written much
later than chapters 1-8. They contain various oracles concerning judgement on Israel's enemies and the blessings in store
for God's people.

Many have stated that Zechariah did not write chapters 9-
14. A helpful summary of the arguments for and against this
is found in *The New Bible Commentary* (Third Edition 1970,
I.V.P. pp. 787-8), and *The Illustrated Bible Dictionary* (1980,
I.V.P. pp. 1678-9). Evangelical scholars believe that there is
no compelling reason to question the fact that Zechariah
wrote the whole prophecy.

There are many recurring phrases and pictures within the
book but as in Haggai, one phrase catches our eye continually: *'the Lord Almighty'* (see chapter 2). In Zechariah 'the
Lord Almighty' occurs some fifty-two times and no less than
eighteen times in chapter 8 alone.

The Messiah foretold

Only one verse from Haggai is quoted in the New Testament
but at least thirty-three portions of Zechariah are quoted in
about fifty different places in the New Testament. Many of
these are in connection with the Lord Jesus Christ, the most
well-known being the description of the triumphal entry into
Jerusalem (Zechariah 9:9).

'Zechariah foretold Christ's coming in lowliness (6:12;
13:7), his rejection and betrayal for thirty pieces of silver
(11:12-13), his crucifixion (struck by the 'sword' of the Lord;
13:7), his priesthood (6:13), his kingship (6:13; 9:9; 14:9,16),
his coming in glory (14:4), his building of the Lord's temple
(6:12-13), his reign (9:10,14) and his establishment of enduring peace and prosperity (3:10; 9:9-10).'[3]

10.
Remember and repent

Please read Zechariah 1:2-6

'We learn by our mistakes' is a phrase that is often quoted. Indeed, it is good when positive use can be made of a minor disaster, but the problem with mistakes is that most of us do not learn from them; we keep doing the same wrong thing over and over again.

The Israelites were no different from us; we sometimes think they were even worse. The history of Israel was one of disobedience to God, eventually followed by repentance, which soon drifted into lethargy and complacency. This was followed by forgetfulness of the Lord's commandments and then disobedience to God.

But God is so gracious. He continually calls his people back to himself and he waits to receive them when they return. Jesus paints a picture of the patience of God when he speaks of the waiting father in Luke 15:11-32. The prodigal son had gone away to a distant country and he squandered his wealth in wild living. What was his father doing all that time? He was waiting for his faithless son to come to his senses and confess, 'Father, I have sinned against heaven and against you. I am no longer worthy to be called your son; make me like one of your hired men.' When the son eventually returned he saw his father was already waiting to receive him. In fact, it would appear that his father saw him first. Why? Because his father was waiting for him, and had been waiting the whole time the son had been absent from home.

In the same way, the word of the Lord that came to Zechariah was a call to the lethargic Jewish builders to return to the Lord and his ways. It was not Zechariah's message; it came straight from the heart of God.

The anger of the Lord

Zechariah starts off his message by stating that God is angry. Literally he is saying, 'The Lord is displeased with displeasure.' He is very angry. This may seem very strange to our ears. If we wanted to bring comfort, help and succour to a people who had been going through great difficulties, would we start off by telling them that God was angry?

If God is a God of love why is he angry? He is angry because their forefathers took no notice of him. They did not obey God's words (1:6). They preferred to listen to the words of men. They behaved as though they were wiser than God. They only wanted to do what God said when it suited them.

It was not that they had forsaken religion. In fact religion was very important to them; they often consulted prophets. However, the prophets they listened to only told them what they wanted to hear; and the words they wanted to hear were not suitable for them at that time. They desired to be told that everything was all right and that they need not change their behaviour patterns, or alter anything else. The prophets they found said to them, 'Peace, peace,' but Jeremiah tells them that these prophets were false.

> 'From the least to the greatest,
>   all are greedy for gain;
> prophets and priests alike,
>   all practise deceit.
> They dress the wound of my people
>   as though it were not serious.
> "Peace, peace," they say,
>   when there is no peace'
>
> (Jeremiah 6:13-14; 8:10-11).

Paul spoke similarly when he said that the days are coming 'when men will not put up with sound doctrine. Instead, to suit their own desires, they will gather around them a great number of teachers to say what their itching ears want to hear' (2 Timothy 4:3).

Zechariah reminded the Jews that God's Word abides for ever. His voice is eternal and his Word endures for all generations to all generations.

God was not only angry because their forefathers did not keep God's words. They did not keep God's decrees either (1:6). When the Lord issues a command it must be obeyed. These Jews did not know the words of John Henry Sammis, but they are very appropriate at this point.

> Trust and obey!
> For there's no other way
> To be happy in Jesus –
> But to trust and obey.

Endeavouring to keep the Ten Commandments is very important for people of all generations. People of every age need to be reminded that these are God's eternal decrees. Moses did not come down from the mountain carrying under his arm 'The Ten Suggestions'!

God's Word is unchanging. God means what he says. The teachings of the Bible have not changed. They do not alter with the fashions of society. We cannot modify the Bible's teaching to fit in with today's moral standards. God did not intend that the principles for living contained in his Word should be adjusted to suit present-day ideals. His Word applies to people of all ages. While in exile the Israelites learnt that they were experiencing God's punishment for disobeying God's commands. God still demands that we follow his decrees and take serious note of his Word.

God was not angry with their forefathers because he wanted to punish and then destroy them. He wanted to bring them to repentance. God shows his love by being fair and just in all his dealings with his people. An earthly father does not love his children if he continually turns a 'blind eye' to their bad behaviour. If he truly loves his child he chastens and corrects him or her. Proverbs 3:11 tells us,

> 'My son, do not despise the Lord's discipline
>   and do not resent his rebuke,
> because the Lord disciplines those he loves,
>   as a father the son he delights in.'

The old proverb says, 'Spare the rod and spoil the child.'

God was angry with their forefathers

He mentions their forefathers three times in these few verses. He says he is **'very angry'** with them (1:2). He states that these returned exiles should not be like their forefathers. **'Do not be like your forefathers, to whom the earlier prophets proclaimed: This is what the Lord Almighty says: "Turn from your evil ways and your evil practices." But they would not listen or pay attention to me, declares the Lord'** (1:4). And he asks in verse 5, **'Where are your forefathers now?'**

Why was God angry with their forefathers? He was angry *because they took no notice of God's Word*. They worshipped other gods. God had said on Mount Sinai, 'You shall not make for yourself an idol in the form of anything in heaven above or on the earth beneath or in the waters below. You shall not bow down to them or worship them; for I, the Lord your God, am a jealous God, punishing the children for the sin of the fathers to the third and fourth generation of those who hate me' (Exodus 20:5). However, they soon made a golden calf and worshipped it; and many, many times they followed the Baal worship of the heathen nations. Jeremiah had reprimanded them for their worship of other gods. He could not understand why a nation who had the only true God as their Lord should want to worship man-made idols. He said,

> '"Has a nation ever changed its gods?
>   (Yet they are not gods at all.)
> But my people have exchanged their Glory
>   for worthless idols.
> Be appalled at this, O heavens,
>   and shudder with great horror,"
>   declares the Lord.
> "My people have committed two sins:
> They have forsaken me,
>   the spring of living water,
> and have dug their own cisterns,
>   broken cisterns that cannot hold water"'

(Jeremiah 2:11-13).

God was also angry with their forefathers *because they ignored his warnings.* God did not just issue the Ten Commandments at Sinai and then leave the people to make of them what they could. He continually warned them about the importance of keeping his law. In Leviticus 26:14-17 he said, 'But if you will not listen to me and carry out all these commands, and if you reject my decrees and abhor my laws and fail to carry out all my commands and so violate my covenant, then I will do this to you: I will bring upon you sudden terror, wasting diseases and fever that will destroy your sight and drain away your life. You will plant seed in vain, because your enemies will eat it. I will set my face against you so that you will be defeated by your enemies; those who hate you will rule over you, and you will flee even when no one is pursuing you.'

Famine was a constant trouble for the Jews. They thought that when they returned from exile the land, having lain fallow for over forty-nine years, would yield an abundant harvest. In actual fact Haggai had to point out to them: 'You have planted much, but have harvested little' (Haggai 1:6). Not only did famine afflict them, but they were ruled over by those they hated; the captivity in Babylon was a painful period for many of them.

Zechariah graciously points out to the Jews that God does keep his word. God was angry with their forefathers because they ignored his warnings, and those who persist in disobedience will be punished until they are brought to their senses.

If we refuse to return to God and to the ways laid down so clearly in the Bible, then we shall have to suffer for it. 'Our God is a consuming fire' (Hebrews 12:29) and he will judge those who refuse to return to him and his ways. 'God is angry with the wicked every day' (Psalm 7:11 AV). '"The Lord will judge his people." It is a dreadful thing to fall into the hands of the living God' (Hebrews 10:30-31). Are we among those who still refuse to acknowledge the Lord and follow his ways? T. V. Moore says, 'The seedlings of life on earth shall be harvested in heaven or hell.'

A third reason why God was angry with their forefathers was *because they were not afraid of his curses,* which he said would descend upon disobedient people. They behaved as though they did not believe that God meant what he said. 'However, if you do not obey the Lord your God and do not carefully follow all his commands and decrees I am giving you today, all these curses will come upon you and overtake you: You will be cursed in the city and cursed in the country. Your basket and your kneading trough will be cursed. The fruit of your womb will be cursed, and the crops of your land, and the calves of your herds and the lambs of your flocks. You will be cursed when you come in and cursed when you go out' (Deuteronomy 28:15-19).

God was angry with their forefathers because they drove him to punish them. It was because of their forefathers' disobedience that the captivity in Babylon took place. Jeremiah and others had warned them that punishment would surely come upon the people unless they mended their ways, but they took no notice. The Second Book of Chronicles tells us why the captivity took place: 'All the leaders of the priests and the people became more and more unfaithful, following all the detestable practices of the nations and defiling the temple of the Lord, which he had consecrated in Jerusalem. The Lord, the God of their fathers, sent word to them through his messengers again and again, because he had pity on his people and on his dwelling-place. But they mocked God's messengers, despised his words and scoffed at his prophets until the wrath of the Lord was aroused against his people and there was no remedy. He brought up against them the king of the Babylonians, who killed their young men with the sword in the sanctuary, and spared neither young man nor young woman, old man or aged. God handed all of them over to Nebuchadnezzar' (2 Chronicles 36:14-17).

As a consequence of their sin against God's words and his decrees they spent about seventy years as prisoners away from their homeland. Through Zechariah, God now reminds this new generation of Jews what had happened to their forefathers. He is saying to them, 'I'm still the same today. I don't forget what I say. And if you also do not mend your ways, then you too will experience my hand in punishment for your sins.' Notice that God does not say, 'I hate your sin.' We often hear it said that God loves the sinner, but hates his sin. He says here, 'I was angry with your forefathers.' God hates sinners! But he loves them to forsake their sins and he is ready to forgive them and, like the father of the prodigal son, he is waiting to receive repentant and returning sinners.

God shows his kindness towards the people

The substance of Zechariah's opening message is contained in verse 3. God says, **'Return to me.'** He gives the weary, unenthusiastic people of God this gracious call. He does not say, 'You are too bad. I don't want anything more to do with you.' He says, 'Return to me.' In effect he is saying, 'Do you see your need? Do you recognize the awful plight you are in? Then return to me.' He is calling them to repentance, and that means they are required to have a change of heart, of mind and of will.

God does not say, 'Return to doing good.' Good works are very desirable and necessary, but God does not first of all call them to return to good works. That is not the message of this prophecy.

He does not say, 'Return to obeying my commandments.' He certainly wants them to do that. Obeying God's laws is vital, but he knows that no one can hope to obey God until they first of all return to the Lord himself. There is no hope for anyone anywhere else than in returning to the Lord Almighty. 'In repentance and rest is your salvation' (Isaiah 30:15).

God does not call the people to return to religious ceremonial, even though they are trying to rebuild the temple. He says, 'If your heart is not right with me, then your devotions can never be acceptable in my sight' (see Haggai 2:14). As we saw in our studies in Haggai, the psalmist said to God,

> 'You do not delight in sacrifice, or I would bring it;
>   you do not take pleasure in burnt offerings.
> The sacrifices of God are a broken spirit;
>   a broken and contrite heart,
>   O God, you will not despise'
>
> (Psalm 51:16-17).

What the Lord is saying is that the only hope for the people is to return to the Lord in whole-hearted contrition and seek his forgiveness. They must show their sorrow for their sin and seek to return to the Lord. They must desire a personal, right relationship with God.

God is waiting to receive them

The Lord Almighty adds this promise: 'If you return to me,
then I will return to you.' God says to these people, 'Your
forefathers have been very wicked. They have set you a bad
example. You have had to suffer terribly, in Babylon,
because of their sin. Now I am giving you the opportunity to
be right with me. If you will but return to me, then I will
return to you.'

Most of their forefathers would not listen or pay attention
to God when he called upon them to turn from their evil ways
and practices (1:4) but there was a godly remnant who did
repent. They said, **'The Lord Almighty has done to us what
our ways and practices deserve, just as he determined to do'**
(1:6).

The call to repent

This message of repentance rings all through the Scriptures. It
was the keynote in the preaching of all the **'earlier prophets'**
(1:4).

> 'Seek the Lord while he may be found;
>   call on him while he is near.
> Let the wicked forsake his way
>   and the evil man his thoughts.
> Let him turn to the Lord, and he will have mercy on him,
>   and to our God, for he will freely pardon'
> (Isaiah 55:6-7).

'Repent! Turn away from all your offences; then sin will not
be your downfall. Rid yourselves of all the offences you have
committed, and get a new heart and a new spirit. Why will you
die, O house of Israel?' (Ezekiel 18:30-31).

Hosea said, 'Return, O Israel, to the Lord your God'
(Hosea 14:1). Joel gave a similar call:

> 'Return to the Lord your God,
>   for he is gracious and compassionate,

> slow to anger and abounding in love,
>   and he relents from sending calamity.
> Who knows? He may turn and have pity
>   and leave behind a blessing'
>
> (Joel 2:12-13).

Amos adds, 'Seek the Lord and live' (Amos 5:6), and
Zephaniah says,

> 'Gather together ... before the fierce anger of the Lord
>   comes upon you,
>   before the day of the Lord's wrath comes upon you.
> Seek the Lord, all you humble of the land ...
>   perhaps you will be sheltered
>   on the day of the Lord's anger'
>
> (Zephaniah 2:2-3).

Despite all these calls to remember the Lord and turn to
him in repentance, the people did not **'listen or pay attention
to me, declares the Lord'** (1:4).

However, Haggai and Zechariah still persisted in calling
the people to return to the Lord, and Malachi, the final Old
Testament prophet, issues the same basic message: '"Return
to me, and I will return to you," says the Lord Almighty'
(Malachi 3:7).

After Malachi ceased his prophesying there were four long
centuries of silence. What broke that silence? The voice of
John the Baptist crying, 'Repent, for the kingdom of heaven
is near' (Matthew 3:1). When Jesus began to preach, his first
public utterance, too, was 'Repent!' (Matthew 4:17), and in
the Great Commission 'repentance' still finds a prominent
place (Luke 24:47). The apostolic preaching likewise contained this same basic element: 'Repent, then, and turn to
God, so that your sins may be wiped out, that times of refresh-
ing may come from the Lord' (Acts 3:19); and 'God ... now ...
commands all people everywhere to repent' (Acts 17:30).

How gracious God is! He forgives those who are truly
repentant and who turn to him in faith. And he saves them
with an everlasting salvation. How sad it is that many reject
Christ because they find his way of salvation too simple for

their proud hearts! They want to earn their salvation rather than casting themselves wholly upon God, seeking his mercy and grace.

Time is quickly passing. **'Where are your forefathers now? And the prophets, do they live for ever?'** (1:5). It is not only the elderly and the infirm who are called to leave this life. Many who are young are killed every day in accidents on the roads and in the home and factory. And others die through painful diseases. We need to ask ourselves, 'Where do I stand with God? If he should call me to leave this life today, where will I spend eternity?' God says to all of us, 'Be like the prodigal son and return to me and I will certainly return to you.' 'Come near to God and he will come near to you' (James 4:8).

And this is made possible because the Lord Jesus Christ went all the way to Calvary to suffer and die, in order to take the punishment that was due to his people because of their sin.

> He died that we might be forgiven,
>   He died to make us good,
> That we might go at last to heaven,
>   Saved by his precious blood.
>
> (Cecil Frances Alexander).

The church must repent

When God makes a promise he always means it and he always keeps it. He is never prevented from fulfilling his promise, nor does he forget it.

So Zechariah concludes his opening address. He is concerned to encourage the people. He wants them to be better builders for God's glory. He desires that they might walk closely with God and honour him in all they do and say and think. But there is a big problem: God's people have sinned.

The church today is not what it should be. There are so many evil ways and wrong practices going on under the name of the Christian religion. Some churches are far too conceited about their own achievements or 'sound teaching'. Some fellowships are jealous of the 'success' of others; and there is much backbiting going on and gloating over the failures of those groups which appear to have departed from the Word of God.

The Lord is saying to his people today, 'You are too self-satisfied, too smug, too self-sufficient and too proud of your own good name. You need to turn away from yourself and turn to me.'

The church at Ephesus was similar to many of God's people in this twentieth century. They were a very hard-working group of people who had the desire and ability to weed out those who were not true apostles. They endured great hardships for the name of their Lord, but despite all their orthodoxy and their zeal for the truth Christ himself calls upon them to repent and return to their first love, otherwise he will remove them (Revelation 2:1-7). When I visited the ruins of Ephesus in 1981 I was told that there were no Christians in the whole district, nor had there been for many centuries.

However pure you think your church fellowship might be, it is still vital to listen and pay attention to the Lord Almighty and return to him in humility and obedience.

11.
Horsemen, horns and hammers

Visions 1 and 2

Please read Zechariah 1:7-21

Three months have passed since Zechariah's first message from God. We have now reached the twenty-fourth day of the eleventh month of the second year of King Darius. Exactly five months earlier the returned exiles had, at last, started work on rebuilding the temple at Jerusalem. This was on 'the twenty-fourth day of the sixth month in the second year of King Darius' (Haggai 1:15).

Less than a month later (on the twenty-first day of the seventh month – Haggai 2:1) the people viewed their handiwork and saw that it was miserable in comparison with the glories of Solomon's temple. As a result of their disappointment, Haggai had preached to them and had encouraged them to press on with the work.

During the following month Zechariah declared his first message from the Lord – the call to repentance (Zechariah 1:1-6). As we have seen, this message was given to encourage the people to return to the Lord and to give greater diligence to the task of building God's house for God's glory. Only clean hands and a pure heart can achieve anything of lasting value for the Lord (Psalm 24:4). We have every reason to believe that Zechariah did not just issue this call to repentance once. Because of the people's attitude he must have kept on ramming the same message home over and over again.

Then notice that it was again on the twenty-fourth day, (this time of the ninth month – exactly two months before Zechariah received his visions) that Haggai delivered both of his final messages (Haggai 2:10,20). That was the turning-point for the Jews in their work of building for God's glory.

God said to them, 'From this day on I will bless you' (Haggai 2:19).

But the people of God were still cast down. Everything seemed to be against them. They had been punished severely in Babylon, and now that they had returned to their own country and were comparatively free, things seemed to be going wrong. The harvest had failed (Haggai 1:6) and they had no enthusiasm for God's work. Were they ever going to be a great nation again? Would God bless them as he had done in the glorious days of King David?

It was at this very time, exactly five months after they had begun work on the Lord's house, that God spoke again.

God spoke using visions (1:7 – 6:8)

These were not dreams; Zechariah was not asleep. He said, **'During the night I had a vision'** (1:8). God chose this fairly new way to reveal his truths to the people. Other prophets in the past had received visions, but not, so far as we know, since the return from Babylon. There are eight visions (nine or ten according to some commentators) in these opening chapters of Zechariah. They build up one upon another until we have a full picture of what God was saying to the Jews at that time. The purpose of these visions was purely to encourage the people to press on with the work of the Lord. They were designed to bring comfort and hope to weary, cast-down souls.

They were not dreams. Dreams can be musings of the mind. They need not, for us, have any real meaning or significance, but Zechariah's visions were genuine enough. They were just as much **'the word of the Lord'** (1:7) as the message of 1:2-6. Also we know they were not dreams because Zechariah had to be wakened up at the beginning of the fifth one (4:1). And throughout he keeps saying things like, 'then I looked up' (1:18; 2:1), 'then he showed me' (3:1), 'I looked again' (5:1; 6:1), 'the angel ... said to me, "Look up and see"' what is happening (5:5).

Those eight visions all appear to have been given in the same night. They are given to encourage those who are 'fed up'. They are given to strengthen those who like Elijah say, 'I have had enough, Lord' (1 Kings 19:4). They are given to enthuse those who are feeling weak and useless.

The first vision (1:7-17)

In this vision the first thing that Zechariah sees is a man. This man is riding a red horse, yet his horse is stationary in the vision. This is because the horse is standing in a hollow – a ravine (1:8). Some say that this is the valley of Kidron just outside of Jerusalem.

The angel of the Lord

Very soon this man is revealed as the angel of the Lord (1:11). We often meet with someone called 'the angel of the Lord' in the Old Testament. Let us look briefly at two accounts of his appearing.

It was the angel of the Lord who spoke to Hagar in Genesis 16:7. He said to her, 'I will so increase your descendants that they will be too numerous to count' (Genesis 16:10). The angel of the Lord was going to do this great thing.

Secondly, when Abraham was about to offer his beloved son Isaac as a sacrifice to God on Mount Moriah, it was the angel of the Lord who called out, 'Do not do anything to him' (Genesis 22:12). This same angel called Abraham from heaven and said, 'I swear by myself, declares the Lord, that because you have done this and have not withheld your son, your only son, I will surely bless you and make your descendants as numerous as the stars in the sky and as the sand on the seashore' (Genesis 22:16-17).

Who then, is this one who appears as a human being and yet is divine? There is only one who fits the description. The angel of the Lord must be the God-man whom the New Testament reveals. The angel of the Lord is none other than the pre-incarnate Christ. He is Jesus revealed in the Old Testament, before he was born as a baby at Bethlehem.

The myrtle trees

Where is the angel of the Lord standing? He is among the

myrtle trees. The myrtle is a common bush in Israel. It is a beautiful shrub with glossy leaves and white star-like clusters of fragrant flowers. A remarkable thing about this myrtle is that its leaves give out a rich, fragrant smell, but only when they are crushed. Apparently myrtle is the basis of the Hebrew name for Esther – *Hadassah* (Esther 2:7).[1]

The myrtle tree was a symbol of Israel. God did not choose a proud cedar tree to stand for the Jews. Nor did he choose an oak with its great strength. No. He chose the lowly myrtle – humble, unpretentious, giving out its sweetest fragrance when it is bruised by the weight of affliction.

Though God's redeemed people, the church, seem at times to be in a hollow – a low place and very insignificant (1:8), yet God is with them and will strengthen and help them. The failures, the disappointments and the losses will all be forgotten when Jesus Christ (the angel of the Lord) is recognized as standing with his people. God says,

> 'Fear not, for I have redeemed you;
>   I have summoned you by name; you are mine.
> When you pass through the waters,
>   I will be with you;
> and when you pass through the rivers,
>   they will not sweep over you.
> When you walk through the fire,
>   you will not be burned;
>   the flames will not set you ablaze.
> For I am the Lord, your God,
>   the Holy One of Israel, your Saviour'
>
> (Isaiah 43:1-3).

More horsemen

Behind the angel of the Lord are riders of other horses – red, brown and white (1:8). Zechariah, having seen the vision, then asks a question. He puts it to another angel (1:9). This angel will become familiar to us, as he appears in all of the other visions too. He is described as **'the angel who was talking with me'**. He acts as Zechariah's interpreter.

Notice the question that Zechariah asks. Speaking of these other horses and horsemen, he asks, **'What are these?'** We would probably have asked, **'Who are these?'** But who they are does not seem to matter very much. The meaning of the colour of the horses is not important either (but red probably stands for war and bloodshed, white for purity and victory, and brown possibly symbolizes a combination of both). We must treat these visions rather like the parables of Jesus. We should remember that they usually teach *one main truth only*; we should not press each detail or try to squeeze every ounce of meaning out of them. Zechariah sees the troops of horses and asks, 'What does this mean?'

The angel of the Lord now speaks directly to Zechariah. He says, **'They are the ones the Lord has sent to go throughout the earth'** (1:10). And, as Zechariah watches, he sees these horsemen reporting directly to the angel of the Lord (who was still standing among the myrtle trees). They give the following information: 'The whole world is at rest and peace' (1:11).

If we read nothing more of this vision we would probably be thrilled to hear such news. Do we not long for peace throughout the world? Surely it is good news that the whole world is at rest and in peace!

But, strangely enough, this answer does not please the angel of the Lord. Who was it that was enjoying peace and security? The nations all around Jerusalem. These nations who had severely treated the Jews for seventy years were enjoying a tranquil existence, while the people of God were still suffering the effects of their years in captivity.

The angel of the Lord pleads for God's people

Then the angel of the Lord (God the Son) speaks to the Lord Almighty (God the Father) and says, **'How long will you withhold mercy from Jerusalem and from the towns of Judah, which you have been angry with these seventy years?'** (1:12). Notice that the angel of the Lord re-echoes the age-old cry of God's people: 'My soul is in anguish. How long, O Lord, how long?' (Psalm 6:3).

Christ is praying for us; and God will hear and answer our prayers both for our good and his glory. Jesus prayed to his Father, 'I am not praying for the world, but for those you have given me, for they are yours' (John 17:9). It is a great blessing for God's people to know that our Saviour is now in heaven, at God's right hand speaking to the Father on our behalf. 'Jesus lives for ever, he has a permanent priesthood. Therefore he is able to save completely those who come to God through him, because he always lives to intercede for them' (Hebrews 7:24-25).

Here in verse 12 is another example of the doctrine of the Trinity in the Old Testament. 'God is one' is the often-repeated declaration of the Jews. 'Hear, O Israel: The Lord our God, the Lord is one' (Deuteronomy 6:4). Yet God is three in one, and one in three. We have a further example in Scripture of God pleading with God. In the garden of Gethsemane Jesus cries to his Father, 'My Father, if it is possible, may this cup be taken from me. Yet not as I will, but as you will' (Matthew 26:39; Mark 14:36; Luke 22:42).

Zechariah's task

As a result of the pleading of the angel of the Lord, **'the Lord spoke kind and comforting words'** to the interpreting angel (1:13). And Zechariah is given an encouraging message to proclaim to the people. 'This is what the Lord Almighty says: "I am very jealous for Jerusalem and Zion, but I am very angry with the nations that feel secure. I was only a little angry, but they added to the calamity"' (1:14-15).

God has ceased to be angry with the Jews. He wants now to show his love for them by making it clear to all the other nations that they are his chosen people. He is jealous for Jerusalem and Zion (i.e. the whole of his redeemed people).

Instead, God is now angry with the strong and secure nations because they have punished the Jews too much. 'They had done their utmost to make the Lord's chastisements – which were to teach his people to put their trust in God, not in man or idols (Isa. 10:20f; Jer. 3:22-25) – an unendurable evil (Isa. 10:5-19; 24). Therefore the anger of the Lord now turns against the heathen, while his full mercies will be restored to Jerusalem.'[2]

It is when the enemies of God seem to be at rest and gloating over God's people that Christ will arise with strength and deliverance for his people.

A Sovereign protector I have,
  Unseen, yet for ever at hand,
Unchangeably faithful to save,
  Almighty to rule and command.
He smiles, and my comforts abound;
  His grace as the dew shall descend,
And walls of salvation surround
  The soul he delights to defend.

                                        (Augustus Toplady).

God's blessings on Jerusalem

In verses 16 and 17 we read of the future prosperity of
Jerusalem. God is going to return to the holy city. As
Zechariah sees the first three visions, he is standing outside of
the city. He sees the angel of the Lord still in the ravine, but
he now receives news that God is to return to Jerusalem. His
temple will be rebuilt to receive him – for God dwells in his
temple. The house of God is very important to him, and
God's plan for his people. The Jews had every reason to
hasten on with its rebuilding, for in a few centuries' time the
Messiah, God's chosen and anointed one, would ride in
triumph into Jerusalem. In Zechariah 9:9 the prophet
describes the scene of the first Palm Sunday:

'Rejoice greatly, O Daughter of Zion!
  Shout, Daughter of Jerusalem!
See, your king comes to you,
  righteous and having salvation,
  gentle and riding on a donkey.'

(Compare this prophecy with Matthew 21:5 and John 12:15.)
  But these verses do not only speak of the temple; they
speak of the city itself. It too, is going to be rebuilt. We will
see more of this when we study chapter 2. God will again
bring honour upon the whole area around Jerusalem, for God
has chosen Jerusalem for himself and his own people.
  We can begin to see how some of this will work out by taking a brief look at the second vision.

The second vision (1:18-21)

Then Zechariah looked up, **'and there before me were four horns!'** (1:18). Horns in the Old Testament always speak of strength and power. We do not see any massive bulls or steers, only their horns. We find similar horns in Daniel 7, but those speak of powers which are to come. Here the four horns are the horns that **'scattered** [past tense] **Judah, Israel and Jerusalem'** (1:19).

There are four of them because they represent powers which are in all four quarters of the globe. The nations which have attacked Jerusalem have come from every direction. Assyria and Chaldea were actually situated to the north-east of Jerusalem, but they entered the land from the north, through Samaria. Egypt lay in the south-west, but invaded Judah from the south.

The Philistines came from the west and Ammon and Moab arrived from the east. (Perhaps we do not know so much about the attacks from the east but see what Zephaniah says about the insults and taunts that they flung against Judah – Zephaniah 2:8).

Then, as Zechariah watches, he sees four powerful craftsmen. **'What are these coming to do?'** he asks his interpreting angel (1:21). We are left in no doubt as to their purpose. **'The craftsmen have come to terrify them** [the horns that scattered Judah] **and throw down these horns of the nations who lifted up their horns against the land of Judah to scatter its people'** (1:21).

Those who once terrified the Jews will themselves be terrified. God will not be put to shame. His people will triumph over all their enemies. God will send those who are best fitted to destroy them. These craftsmen have mighty hammers (whether they are powerful carpenters or strong blacksmiths) and they will utterly destroy the enemies of God and his people. And these craftsmen will not only destroy all of Judah's enemies then present, but they will crush all future enemies of God's people. '[Christ] must reign until he has put all his enemies under his feet' (1 Corinthians 15:25).

God's people will triumph

These visions were addressed to God's people of old. The same God still speaks the same kind of words of comfort and strength to his people today. Those who are fearful that the enemies of God will crush the church need to give serious attention to the message of Zechariah. Do not be tempted to think that the powers of evil are too mighty for God's people in the twentieth century. The Lord has raised up a craftsman who is so strong that he will crush all the enemies of his people and will gain victory over them. Remember that Paul did not write his epistles to a few super-saints who had special faith to enable them to fight against their enemies. He wrote them to Christian fellowships, many of them small and struggling. And he asked, 'Who shall separate us from the love of Christ? Shall trouble or hardship or persecution or famine or nakedness or danger or sword? As it is written: "For your sakes we face death all day long; we are considered as sheep to be slaughtered." No, in all these things we are more than conquerors through him who loved us' (Romans 8:35-37). '"Where, O death, is your victory? Where, O death, is your sting?" The sting of death is sin, and the power of sin is the law. But thanks be to God! He gives us the victory through our Lord Jesus Christ' (1 Corinthians 15:55-57).

12.
The holy city

Vision 3

Please read Zechariah 2:1-13

This third vision continues with the theme of God's choice of
Jerusalem and his protection of it. God shows Zechariah that
he is with his people and that he has a plan and a purpose for
Zion (his holy city and his holy people).

The description of Jerusalem (2:1-5)

Jerusalem is often in the news today. It is a divided city. There
are Jews living in it. To be a Jew means that you have been
born of a Jewish mother and have been circumcised and
declared to be a member of the Jewish race. It can also mean
that you follow the Jewish religion which is based on the law
of Moses and the teaching of the Talmud. For many today
who are living in Jerusalem, the nationalistic aspect is much
more important than the religious one. The sad thing about
most Jews is that they still refuse to accept that the Messiah
has come. For them Jesus is not the Christ. They are still looking for a deliverer to come, God's anointed one.

There are also Arabs living in Jerusalem. These follow the
teaching of the Islamic religion which says that Jesus was a
great prophet, but not the Son of God.

There are some Christians in Jerusalem too. They come
from all nations. They believe that Jesus is God's chosen one
who has come to set his people free from their sin.

Jerusalem is the Holy City of three major world religions.
It is revered by millions. It is regarded as a place where God
has especially set his favour. It is a city to which millions of pilgrims flock each year.

Yet it is a place of violence. Several people have been mur-
dered in recent years near the great mosque which beautifies
the Jerusalem skyline, the Dome of the Rock. This stands on
Temple Mount. The whole raised area around the mosque is
the site of the house of God. It was here that Abraham nearly
offered Isaac as a sacrifice to God. It was here that David
purchased the threshing-floor of Araunah. It was here that
Solomon built his magnificent golden temple. It was here that
Zerubbabel laboured to rebuild the house of the Lord. It was
on this same spot that Jesus was taken as an eight-day-old
child to be circumcised, and within the courts of this temple
Jesus did much of his teaching and preaching. And it was
here, in A.D. 70, that Titus and his Roman army utterly
destroyed the house of the Lord, so that not one stone stood
upon another (Matthew 24:2).

One of the many pictures we have of the people of God in
the Bible is that of a city, the new Jerusalem. This city is
described in great detail. 'There is a river whose streams
make glad the city of God' (Psalm 46:4). 'It is beautiful in its
loftiness, the joy of the whole earth' (Psalm 48:1-2). 'Glorious
things are said of you, O city of God' (Psalm 87:3). Revelation 22 describes the city of God and says the river of the
water of life flows down the middle of its streets, the tree of
life yields its fruit every month, there is no longer any curse
and it has no need of any sun or light because the Lord God
will give all the light that is needed.

> City of God, how broad and far
>   Outspread thy walls sublime!
> The true thy chartered freemen are,
>   Of every age and clime.
>
> (S. Johnson)

Now, in this third vision, God shows Zechariah what his
intention is for this city of Jerusalem.

A man with a measuring line

Zechariah looked and saw before him **'a man with a measuring line in his hand'** (2:1). He asked the man where he was

going. The man replied that he was going to measure Jerusalem to find out how wide and how long it was.

How could he do that? Jerusalem had lain in ruins for many years. It was almost impossible to determine where the boundaries of the city should be. History tells us that it would be another seventy-five years before Nehemiah would rebuild the walls of the city. So what city was this man (probably the angel of the Lord) going to measure?

From what follows we learn that this vision was not about the earthly city of Jerusalem, but the new Jerusalem. In Galatians 4 Paul writes about Hagar and Sarah, the mothers of Abraham's two sons. He says that these two women represent two covenants, one of slavery and one of freedom: 'Now Hagar stands for Mount Sinai in Arabia and corresponds to the present city of Jerusalem, because she is in slavery with her children. But the Jerusalem which is above is free, and she is our mother' (Galatians 4:25-26).

The new Jerusalem

This city of Jerusalem (the new Jerusalem) is a picture of the people of God, the church, with the Lord dwelling in their midst. Just as the barrier in the temple, which separated between Jew and non-Jew, was to be thrown down (Ephesians 2:14), so Christ will come and break down every barrier and let all true believers, of whatever natural race, come into the very presence of the Lord Almighty.

While Zechariah was speaking to the man with the measuring line, another angel came to the interpreting angel and said, **'Run, tell that young man, "Jerusalem will be a city without walls because of the great number of men and livestock in it. And I myself will be a wall of fire around it," declares the Lord, "and I will be its glory within"'** (2:4-5).

There is some urgency about what happened next. The interpreting angel is told to 'run' and give a message to the young man, that is, to Zechariah. 'Those who perform God's will must not merely creep nor walk, but run with alacrity.'[1] What was this important message? Jerusalem will have no city walls. This must have amazed Zechariah. This was unheard of. How would it protect itself? What would happen if enemies came against it? God himself supplies the answer to these questions.

Jerusalem's security outside and inside

'I myself will be a wall of fire around it' (2:5). Just as Elisha was protected by a wall of fire at Dothan (2 Kings 6:17), just as the children of Israel were guided and protected by a pillar of fire, so God will defend his holy city, the people of God, and keep them safe from all attacks by their enemies.

It was then revealed that the reason why the new Jerusalem will have no walls is because of the vast number of its inhabitants. Not only will many, many people live in Zion ('city of our God') but their cattle will take up much room also. Laetsch says that 'Cattle here represents all the possessions, the wealth of the city.'[2]

Not only will the new Jerusalem have God as a wall of fire around it, but God himself will be its glory within. And, if God is with his people, what glory that will be! 'I am with you' was the message God gave through Haggai when the people commenced in earnest the rebuilding of the temple (Haggai 1:13). It is the message constantly given to encourage and strengthen God's people down through the ages. It is the comfort of every believer that one day he or she will experience the glory of God in the heavenly Jerusalem.

The call to the exiled Jews (2:6-9)

There were still many Jews living in Babylon. Zerubbabel (or Sheshbazzar)[3] had brought back with him many thousands of Jews, but many still remained in Babylon. Why was that?

It may be that they refused to believe that God would again bless Jerusalem; their unbelief had kept them in the land of their captivity. Perhaps they could not face the hard work of rebuilding the house and city of God; they had grown flabby in the land of their exile. Some may have been unwilling to fight against the enemies of Judah; many did not return to God's city because they did not have the stamina to put on the whole armour of God (Ephesians 6:10-18) and fight against

Satan and all his hosts. Maybe they were suspicious of the decrees of Cyrus and Darius; they wanted cast iron guarantees of success before they would venture out in the work of the Lord. They lacked the faith to launch out into the unknown; they did not believe that God would protect and help them. Some, no doubt, had been in Babylon so long that they had forgotten how wonderful Jerusalem really was. And some must have contrasted their comfortable life-style, and the wealth that they had amassed in Babylon, with the ruins of Jerusalem and the sheer hard work that would be required of them if they returned to the holy land; they were not prepared to give up the comforts of the present for the blessings of the future.

The urgency of the call

Notice the tone of the language: **'"Come! Come! Flee from the land of the north,'** declares the Lord (2:6). It is God himself who says this. He calls them to **'escape'** (1:7). He wants his chosen people to forsake the **'Daughter of Babylon'** (1:7); that means they must leave the city and people of Babylon. He wants them to return to enjoy the blessings he has in store for Jerusalem and the people of God. Notice how he pleads with them to return to their real home.

God's people today are called to 'come out from them and be separate' (2 Corinthians 6:17). Believers are altogether out of place when they live with, and enjoy the pleasures of, the world. Just as many in Zechariah's time no doubt gave excuses for remaining in Babylon, so many backsliding Christians give numerous excuses for not returning to the Lord and his ways. It costs some a great deal to have the courage to return to the Lord.

Those who are happy to 'dwell in the tents of the wicked' (Psalm 84:10) become dulled in their consciences. They forget what a blessing it is to be among the people of God. They enjoy the excitement and garish toys of the world, forgetting that these things will soon pass away. But God graciously calls his wandering people to escape from the influence of Satan and worldly pleasures, and to return to him and his ways.

In this vision we see that God wants the wayward ones to return, not just to receive the blessings of Jerusalem, but because he is going to punish the nations and he wants them out of the 'firing- line'. The nations had treated God's people too badly.

God had punished the Jews by allowing the Babylonians (and others) to take them away to their own lands, but he did not intend that his people should be so cruelly treated. Now these oppressors are to suffer for the evil they carried out. God is going to raise his hand against them (2:9). God's hand is powerful. It is almighty. No one can withstand its force. How will God show his hand? The slaves of the nations will **'plunder them'** (2:9). This literally happened in Babylon and in many other places in the days that followed. Spartacus was not the only slave to revolt against the cruel tyranny of his masters. 'History records that Babylon revolted twice during Darius' reign and twice was reconquered. The first revolt seems to have occurred around the time Zechariah was ministering, the second some six years later. Both occasions were times of terrible suffering.'[4]

The 'apple of God's eye'

The nations are to be punished because they have touched God's people. These are called **'the apple of [God's] eye'** (2:8). 'How dearly the welfare of his people concerns the Lord. It is here stated thus: "He that touches you touches the apple of his eye." Because whatever touches the eyeball is felt to be very painful, and every man sedulously guards this organ, therefore is this figure chosen. The rash handling of Israel pains God, and, therefore, he protects his people.'[5]

The pupil of the eye is the most precious part and it is natural to shield it from every speck of defilement. Those who wear contact lenses know the pain dust can cause in the eye. God speaks of guarding his people as 'the apple of his eye' in Psalm 17:8 and Proverbs 7:2. He spoke of his care for Israel like this:

'The Lord's portion is his people,
    Jacob his allotted inheritance.

In a desert land he found him,
in a barren and howling waste.
He shielded him and cared for him;
he guarded him as the apple of his eye,
like an eagle that stirs up its nest
and hovers over its young,
that spreads its wings to catch them
and carries them on its pinions'

(Deuteronomy 32:9:11).

Those who dare to attack God's precious possessions will surely be punished.

A place for all nations (2:10-13)

The Jerusalem of Zechariah's time did, eventually, have walls; the remains of some are still there today. But the Jerusalem of the vision had no walls because it will be host to a vast number of new citizens. **'Many nations will be joined with the Lord'** (2:11). If they are to be joined with the Lord then they will have to become new people. They will have to be changed. They will have to become those whom the Lord calls 'my people'. Hosea called one of his sons Lo-Ammi. 'For you are not my people, and I am not your God', but in the next verse we read, 'Yet the Israelites will be like the sand on the seashore, which cannot be measured or counted. In the place where it was said to them, "You are not my people", they will be called "sons of the living God"' (Hosea 1:9-10). Peter says that because of Christ's atoning death upon the cross, 'Now you are the people of God; once you had not received mercy, but now you have received mercy' (1 Peter 2:10).

Isaiah had already spoken of this:

'In the last days
the mountain of the Lord's temple will be established
as chief among the mountains;
it will be raised above the hills,
and all nations will stream to it.
Many peoples will come and say,

"Come, let us go up to the mountain of the Lord,
   to the house of the God of Jacob"'

(Isaiah 2:2-3).

How can all these unclean people from heathen nations approach the holy city? They can only ascend the hill of the Lord if they have clean hands and pure hearts (Psalm 24:3-4). So they must be cleansed from their defilement. The next vision (in chapter 3) will speak more specifically about this.

The New Testament tells us that only the Lord Jesus Christ can justify us and make us right with him. It is only through faith in Christ alone that anyone can inhabit this new Jerusalem. It is all summed up in Revelation 21:1-3: 'Then I saw a new heaven and a new earth, for the first heaven and the first earth had passed away, and there was no longer any sea. I saw the Holy City, the new Jerusalem, coming down out of heaven from God, prepared as a bride beautifully dressed for her husband. And I heard a loud voice from the throne saying, "Now the dwelling of God is with men, and he will live with them. They will be his people, and God himself will be with them and be their God."'

Be still before the Lord

No wonder Zechariah preaches, **'Be still before the Lord, all mankind, because he has roused himself from his holy dwelling'** (2:13). God is going to do mighty things for his people. Jerusalem (that is, all of its inhabitants) deserved to be left to rot because of their forgetfulness of the Lord and his commandments; but he says, **'The Lord will inherit Judah as his portion in the holy land and will again choose Jerusalem'** (2:12). God's mercy to undeserving people is called 'grace' in the New Testament. This is exactly what is promised to the citizens of the new Jerusalem.

How often are we still before the Lord? Do we realize what he is going to do? He is going to punish his enemies with an everlasting punishment. He has roused himself to do just that. We should be still before the Lord and consider our position before him today. The whole of Psalm 46 is relevant to this third vision of Zechariah. Verses 9 and 10 say,

> '"Be still, and know that I am God;
>   I will be exalted among the nations,
>   I will be exalted in the earth."
> The Lord Almighty is with us;
>   the God of Jacob is our fortress.'

The glory of the church

Something of the glory of the church of Jesus Christ is seen in this vision. Local church fellowships are but small manifestations of the one true church, represented by the holy city of Jerusalem. But in the gatherings of God's people his glory can, from time to time, be experienced in a wonderful way. People living on our estate sometimes say, 'How can you worship God in a community hall which is used for all kinds of non-Christian things during the week?' The answer is 'Come and see.' For Jesus said, 'Where two or three come together in my name [even in a hall sometimes used for bingo], there am I with them' (Matthew 18:20). 'It should not be in the splendid cathedrals and gorgeous vestments, and the swell of music, and the glitter of eloquence, but in the indwelling glory of the invisible God.'[6]

As 'many nations will be joined with the Lord in that day' (2:11), so we should be prepared to welcome all whom God is calling into his church. We should not be too hesitant to receive people into the church from all kinds of traditions. If God has called them by his grace, then he will teach them his ways (Micah 4:2). One day the earth 'will be full of the knowledge of the Lord as the waters cover the sea' (Isaiah 11:9). By his blood Jesus Christ purchased men for God 'from every tribe and language and people and nation' (Revelation 5:9).

13.
The great representative

Please read Zechariah 3:1-10

One of Satan's chief purposes in this world is to try to convince everyone that he does not exist. He likes us to think of him as some vague spirit drifting around, causing a few little annoyances from time to time. He is highly delighted when we think of him as a figure of fun with a forked tail and horns coming out of his head. And he enjoys it most when we behave as though he were a figment of our imagination.

He likes us to ignore him so he can be undisturbed as he gets on with his evil work of disrupting the building up of God's kingdom. One of his most effective weapons, one which we all delight to employ, is the human tongue. We are only too ready to gossip about one another. The world enjoys reading scandal about the private lives of soap opera 'stars' or politicians. The church enjoys passing on tittle-tattle about the faults and foibles of its members.

The setting of the vision

The first three visions took place outside Jerusalem. Now the scene moves into the city. The setting of the fourth and fifth visions has reference to the temple. We see Satan standing, as in a court of law, as an accuser. Indeed he is called 'the accuser of our brothers' (Revelation 12:10). As we have the description of him, it seems that he has been casting doubt on the value of God's people. Neither Satan nor Joshua utters a single word in this vision, yet they both play an important role in it.

The returned Jewish exiles had attempted to rebuild the

temple, but they had met much opposition. The Samaritans, the Persian government and others had all done their best to interfere with the building up of God's house. Now we see that Satan had a hand in it too.

The figure of Joshua

Joshua was the high priest in Zechariah's time. We learn this from Haggai 1:1 and Ezra 5:2. We shall meet him again in Zechariah 6:11. He is given his full title in verses 1 and 8 of chapter 3. As we view him, he is standing in a court of law.

Joshua had returned with Zerubbabel from the Babylonian captivity. He had tried to serve his people well, and he had been responsible for the worship of God for many years. He had also been in charge of the spiritual well-being of the Jewish people.

In verse 1 we see Joshua standing before the angel of the Lord, as representative of the Jewish people. As high priest, he always represented them before the Lord. He interceded on their behalf. He pleaded for God's forgiveness for the people's sin, especially when he entered the Holy of Holies once each year on the Day of Atonement (Leviticus 16).

But he stands here in shame. It seems that Satan, who stood at his right hand (in the position of counsel for the prosecution) had been making serious charges against God's people. It appears that he had been reminding the Jews that they had sinned grievously against the Lord. That was very true; Satan often speaks the truth in order to gain our attention and to lure us into the direction he wants us to go: that is, away from God. He tells us that we are sinners of the vilest kind and he tempts us to give up following the Lord because we make such a mess of it.

Whenever we stand before the Lord to seek acceptance for ourselves or others, Satan stands up to resist our prayers. But as we have Satan as an adversary, so we have the Lord Jesus Christ as our Advocate to intercede on our behalf (1 John 2:1).

Another accusation that Satan probably made was that the priests had been unfaithful to their calling and that the people had lost respect for them. There was a large measure of truth in that insinuation too. This would, no doubt, lead on to the reason why they came back to the Holy Land – the rebuilding of the temple. We can almost hear Satan taunting them: 'What a shabby building this is! It's nothing like Solomon's glorious building. Don't you know the heathen are laughing at your poor efforts? This is a disgrace to God. Why don't you give up? Surely it's better to do nothing than give shoddy workmanship to God?'

From this it seems likely that Satan went on to infer that they could not expect God to forgive them and have mercy upon them. Because they were in such a hopeless position, they ought to give up building the temple. Moore puts it like this: 'Enjoy sin at least if you cannot enjoy holiness.'[1]

As Satan proceeds with his accusation, we need to stop and think lest we be carried away by his silver-tongued utterances. What right had Satan to say such things? No wonder God reprimands him with a double 'rebuke' in verse 2.

Notice that during all the accusations of Satan, Joshua remains silent. 'This implies that he has nothing to say by way of defence; silence in the face of charges usually signifies guilt. Nor does God proclaim Joshua's innocence, for such a proclamation was apparently impossible. Yet the Lord can save the case of Joshua.'[2]

God also says that Joshua is a **'burning stick snatched from the fire'**. He means that Joshua had barely escaped from the fires of punishment in Babylon and that God has received him because he has a purpose for him to fulfil (see Amos 4:11).

Joshua's clothes

Joshua's shame is shown by the filthy clothes that he wore (3:3). Filth always represents sin. Satan wants us to see sin as exciting, full of pleasure and wonderful. But God does not see it that way at all. He sees sin as that which separates people from himself. Even our good works are filthy in God's sight: 'All of us have become like one who is unclean, and all our righteous acts are like filthy rags' (Isaiah 64:6).

God is holy and he cannot look upon the filth and defilement that sin brings. If anyone is to stand before God he must wear clean clothes. That does not mean he must always wear a smart suit when he attends church (as a Sikh must bathe and put on clean clothing before handling the *Guvu Granth Sahib,* the Sikh holy book). It does mean that before anyone approaches God, who is holy, he himself must seek to be pure and upright in every way. Jesus said that those who are pure in heart will see God (Matthew 5:8). God cannot look upon sin, so if sinners are to come to him someone else must act on their behalf.

At that point something wonderful happens. The angel of the Lord commands the other angels to take off Joshua's filthy clothes. This leaves him naked. That is how each one of us comes into this world. That is how we all have to appear before God. He looks at us as we really are. 'Nothing in all creation is hidden from God's sight. Everything is uncovered and laid bare before the eyes of him to whom we must give account' (Hebrews 4:13).

We cannot cover up our sin by the rich apparel of good works or religious ceremonial. No. God says, 'It has all got to be removed.' In other words, there is nothing that we can do to gain or merit God's salvation. We can only cast ourselves upon God's mercy and seek his forgiveness and his salvation.

Salvation is all of grace. We are saved not by our own effort, but because God has chosen us in Christ 'before the creation of the world' (Ephesians 1:4). Satan's attacks upon God's people are dealt with by God saying, 'I have chosen Jerusalem' (3:2; 1:17, 2:12). He means, 'I have set my electing love upon my people.' Jesus said, 'You did not choose me, but I chose you' (John 15:16). In the removal of Joshua's filthy clothes God was saying, **'See, I have taken away your sin'** (3:4).

But Joshua is not left standing naked. The angel of the Lord (Jesus Christ himself) says, **'I will put rich garments on you'** (3:4). Joshua could not save himself (and all the people he represented) but God could, and God does. He takes away their filthy clothes (sin) and reclothes them with rich garments (righteousness). These symbolize acceptance and holiness. When the prodigal son returned home in repentance and contrition he discovered that his father was already waiting for him. One of the first acts of his father was to call for the 'best robe and put it on him' (Luke 15:22). Paul exhorts believers to 'clothe yourselves with the Lord Jesus Christ'

(Romans 13:14). He says of Christ, 'God made him who had no sin to be sin for us, so that in him we might become the righteousness of God' (2 Corinthians 5:21).

Count Zinzendorf expresses it like this:

> Jesus, thy robe of righteousness
> My beauty is, my glorious dress;
> 'Midst flaming worlds, in this arrayed,
> With joy shall I lift up my head.
>
> Bold shall I stand in that great day,
> For who aught to my charge shall lay?
> While through thy blood absolved I am
> From sin and fear, from guilt and shame.

The restoration of Joshua

Zechariah is so elated at this wonder of forgiveness and reinstatement that he himself intrudes into the vision and calls out, **'Put a clean turban on his head'** (3:5). This they did, while the angel of the Lord stood by. God approved of the restoration of Joshua to his office of high priest. We read of the high priest's head-dress in the Pentateuch. Exodus 28:36 tells us that it had written across the front of it: 'Holy to the Lord.' Joshua's renewed task is now to intercede before the throne of God on behalf of the people.

In this restored state Joshua is given this charge: **'This is what the Lord Almighty says: "If you will walk in my ways and keep my requirements, then you will govern my house and have charge of my courts, and I will give you a place among these standing here"'** (3:7). Joshua must live a holy life: 'Walk in my ways.' Not only is he to live a good moral life; he is also to carry out his priestly duties diligently: 'Keep my requirements.' He must not give way to Satan's insinuations. He must learn, like the one he prefigures, to say, 'Away from me, Satan!' (Matthew 4:10). He must minister in the house of the Lord and lead the people aright in their walk with God. Then he will be fully restored to his full office of priesthood again. 'If Joshua and his associates are faithful, they will be co-workers with the angels in carrying out God's purposes for Zion and Israel.'[3]

Jesus as our representative stands in our place to take the punishment which was due to us because of our sin. As Joshua stood in filthy rags in the place of all the people, and did not speak a word in his defence, so Jesus stood condemned in our place and bore the guilt of our sin in his own body. He too, when accused, remained silent (Mark 14:61).

What God promises for his people

In his vision, Zechariah sees the Lord calling all the priests to consider what he is going to do (3:8). He says that Joshua and the other priests are symbolic of things to come. Joshua is not only representative of the sinful people of God, but he is a picture of the great High Priest who is to come, the Lord Jesus Christ (Hebrews 10:21); and his fellow priests are symbolic of those who will be priests in the gospel age, that is every true believer (Revelation 1:6).

He then speaks of the Messiah whom he is **'going to bring'**. He calls him **'my servant, the Branch'**. The 'servant' is a title which is often used of the Lord Jesus Christ. We have the servant songs in Isaiah, especially in chapter 53; and in Isaiah 42:1-4 we read,

'Here is my servant, whom I uphold,
    my chosen one in whom I delight;
I will put my Spirit on him
    and he will bring justice to the nations.
He will not shout or cry out,
    or raise his voice in the streets.
A bruised reed he will not break,
    and a smouldering wick he will not snuff out.
In faithfulness he will bring forth justice;
    he will not falter or be discouraged
till he establishes justice on earth..
    In his laws the islands will put their hope.'

The Messiah is also called 'the Branch', or shoot. This is the

one who is going to come. He is not much to look at, at first.
He is 'a root out of dry ground' (Isaiah 53:2); but he will come
as a king to rule in righteousness.

> '"The days are coming," declares the Lord,
>   "when I will raise up to David a righteous Branch,
> a King who will reign wisely
>   and do what is just and right in the land.
> In his days Judah will be saved
>   and Israel will dwell in safety.
> This is the name by which he will be called:
>   The Lord Our Righteousness"'
>
>   (Jeremiah 23:5-6).

What a perfect description of Jesus, who was born of the
'house and line of David'! (Luke 2:4).

The stone set before Joshua

This **'stone'** in verse 9 has given rise to different interpret-
ations. A stone is undoubtedly one of the descriptions of the
Messiah but this prophecy and that of Haggai are taken up
with the rebuilding of the temple. Many stones were used in
that project. When Zechariah saw these visions the foundation of God's house had already been laid (Ezra 3:10), and
in the next vision Zerubbabel will bring out the capstone
(4:7). The Messiah had been promised some time in the
future: **'I am going to bring my servant, the Branch.'** But in
verse 9 the Lord says, **'See, the stone I have [already] set in
front of Joshua.'** This is evidently something different from
the Messiah; therefore, as stones are used in the temple it
must represent the temple of God, his people – the church.

On this stone are seven eyes. In Scripture seven always
speaks of perfection. Some say that this stone has seven facets
upon it (see NIV footnote) but Laetsch[4] and Leupold[5] say that
these seven eyes of the Lord (see 4:10) rest upon the church
as God cares for, and watches over, his people. God is going
to engrave an inscription on this stone. This inscription may
be the name of the Lord. It may indicate that God still has
much work of chiselling to do on the stone to make it fit the

purposes he has for it, or it may signify that the names of his elect will be engraved upon it. But this stone, symbolizing **'this land,'** (God's people) will have its sin removed from it.

Removal of sin in a single day

Zechariah is told that there will be one particular day coming when the sin of the land will be taken away. **'I will remove the sin of this land in a single day'** (3:9). This can be none other than the day of the crucifixion of the Lord Jesus Christ. On that day each of his elect people will have their sin dealt with. And we, who look back to that day remember with joy that great deliverance wrought for us upon the cross at Calvary.

On the Day of Atonement the high priest of the Old Testament had to enter into the Holy of Holies to plead for the forgiveness of his people's sin. This ceremony had to be repeated continually year after year. How different was the atoning sacrifice of Christ's death on that 'single day'! 'Christ did not enter a man-made sanctuary that was only a copy of the true one; he entered heaven itself, now to appear for us in God's presence. Nor did he enter heaven to offer himself again and again, the way the high priest enters the Most Holy Place every year with blood that is not his own. Then Christ would have had to suffer many times since the creation of the world. But now he has appeared once for all at the end of the ages to do away with sin by the sacrifice of himself' (Hebrews 9:24-26).

Because of that wonderful single day, each of God's people know peace, contentment and the blessings of security in Christ; they have peace with God because their sin has been dealt with at Calvary. This vision ends with the quotation of a proverb which for the Jew symbolizes contentment: **'"In that day each of you will invite his neighbour to sit under his vine and fig tree," declares the Lord Almighty'** (3:10, cf. Micah 4:4).

The call to holy living

The church today, like Joshua and his fellow priests, needs to seek to honour the Lord in all its beliefs and practices. God's people are required to live holy lives. When did you last hear, or preach, a clear call for believers to be fully consecrated to the Lord? Individuals and churches need to remember that the world is watching all their actions and trying to discern all their motives. Satan is always waiting to find fault so that he may accuse the followers of Jesus Christ of wrong-doing.

And does that holy living reach out to other people? Is your church a welcoming church? Is the fellowship so rich and so God-honouring that all the fellowship are active in inviting their neighbours to come and 'sit under our vine or fig tree'? (3:10). Satan will try to tell us that we have no blessings to share with others because we are lost on account of our sin. We must reply, 'God doesn't overlook our sin. He has taken it away when he died for his people on the cross of Calvary and now, through repentance and faith we each have been set free. Christ has removed our guilt and clothed us with the Lord Jesus Christ.' Individually we can all say,

> Wounded for me!
> Wounded for me!
> There on the cross
> He was wounded for me:
> Gone my transgressions,
> And now I am free,
> All because Jesus
> Was wounded for me.

(W. G. Ovens)

14.
God-given power

Please read Zechariah 4:1-14

Through the visions given to Zechariah, the people were to be
encouraged to continue with the rebuilding of the temple.
The message was that God was going to destroy the enemies
of his people and again build up a city for the habitation of
those whom he had chosen for himself. The Lord promised
that their sin would be taken away 'in a single day' (3:9) and
that they would all be clothed in righteous garments fit for the
presence of God.

But still the problem remained: how were they, in their
weak state, going to achieve anything of value for God's
glory? By way of an answer to this the Jews were encouraged
by a further vision. Unlike the earlier ones, this one takes
place inside the temple.

It seems that Zechariah had been so overcome with the
wonder and glory of the previous visions on that unforget-
table night that he had drifted off into a 'holy daze'. He said,
'The angel who talked with me returned and wakened me, *as*
a man is wakened from his sleep' (4:1). He had not been
asleep, but he knew of no other way to describe the jolt which
he had received to bring him back to reality.

The interpreting angel asked Zechariah, **'What do you
see?'** (4:2). He was to be asked the same question in 5:2. The
point is that God gave him these visions so that he might see
them and *understand* them. The same idea is expressed by a
child who, having had his teacher explain to him on many
occasions how a sum is worked out, suddenly calls out, 'Oh,
I see it now!'

What Zechariah saw

He saw a golden lampstand (4:3). This was not unfamiliar to
the Jews. Zechariah would recognize it from the temple. In
the tabernacle and the temple had stood a *menorah* – a seven-
branched lampstand. This is one of the symbols of the state of
Israel today (the other being the Star of David).

This particular lampstand had a bowl on the top of it, but,
unlike the *menorah* in the tabernacle or the temple, it also had
two olive trees growing by it, **'one on the right of the bowl and
the other on its left'** (4:3). This was unusual because the olive
trees supplied a continual flow of golden oil to the bowl above
the lampstand (4:12). Somehow the olives grew and were
automatically crushed, and the oil drained into the bowl
above the lampstand.

The symbolism of the vision

The lampstand was golden, and the oil was golden in colour,
too (4:12). Gold is something which is pure, precious and
indestructible. Calvin says that God does not need earthly
wealth or riches, but, 'As we cannot otherwise understand
what exceeds the things of the world, the Lord, under the
figure of gold and silver and precious stones, sets forth those
things which are celestial.'[1]

There were seven branches and seven channels to the
lights. Some commentators say that there were seven channels to each of the seven lights. That makes forty-nine in all.
Leupold tells us that we should not worry that 'The vision is
encumbered with an excess of plumbing. But ... many pipes
did not clutter up the vision nor mar its beauty.'[2] This repeti-
tion of the number seven symbolizes perfection and com-
pleteness. I often remind schoolchildren that seven days
make *one complete week*.

It is clear that the lampstand is a picture of the church of
Jesus Christ. From Revelation 1-3 we learn that lampstands
symbolize the seven churches which, in turn, stand for the
universal church of Jesus Christ. In Revelation 1:12-20 we
share John's vision of someone like a son of man, surrounded
by seven golden lampstands. This person describes himself as

'the First and the Last. I am the Living One; I was dead, and
behold I am alive for ever and ever! And I hold the keys of
death and Hades.' John is told, among other things, that 'The
seven lampstands are the seven churches.'

The whole picture has to do with displaying pure, wholesome light. We think nothing of pressing a light switch so that
we can see; we turn on the light. But until recent centuries
lighting up a dark place required much more effort. Think of
what it must have cost, in time and energy, to maintain the
candelabra in the temple. It was always alight. People were
busily employed to keep the oil topped up, to make sure that
none of the seven lamps went out (Exodus 27:20-21; 30:7-8).
But here, without any human aid, there is a continuous
stream of oil coming straight from the branches of the two
olive trees (4:12) and flowing into the bowl.

Think about the many places in Scripture where we read
about the need for light. We need light to show up the dangerous places, to prevent us from falling (Psalm 27:1). We need
light to shine upon our pathway so that we can see where we
are going (Psalm 119:105). Where can we get that light? Only
from Jesus. He said, 'I am the light of the world. Whoever follows me will never walk in darkness, but will have the light of
life' (John 8:12).

However, Jesus also said, '*You* are the light of the world.'
He went on, 'A city on a hill cannot be hidden. Neither do
people light a lamp and put it under a bowl. Instead they put
in on its stand, and it gives light to everyone in the house. In
the same way, let your light shine before men, that they may
see your good deeds and praise your Father in heaven'
(Matthew 5:14-16). Paul also said that we should 'shine like
stars in the universe as [we] hold out the word of life' (Philippians 2:15-16).

This golden lampstand therefore represents God's people,
individually and collectively, in the act of bearing witness to
the gospel of salvation.

We are urged to hold out the light of God's Word. Just as
the Jews in Zechariah's time were to be witnesses to God by
rebuilding the temple, the place of light, so God's people, the
church, are to be his witnesses today by reaching out to others
with the gospel of salvation. We have a solemn responsibility
to God to be light-bearers in this dark world. We do this not

just by giving money for missionary work, but by our churches being actively and outwardly evangelistic.

The meaning of the vision

Zechariah spoke up. Even though he was a prophet, he did not understand. So he asked the interpreting angel for an explanation (4:4), and, in return, was himself asked a question: **'Do you not know what these are?'** He quickly answered, **'No my Lord'** (4:5); but even then he did not finally get his answer until verse 14.

God desires that we should ask him about things we do not understand. We cannot all have brilliant intellects or a university education. James tells us, 'If any of you lacks wisdom, he should ask God, who gives generously to all without finding fault, and it will be given him' (James 1:5). Do not say, 'We can't believe because we can't understand.' Turn to God and say, 'What do these things mean, Lord?' He is the best one to interpret our problem and give us the solution to it.

Zechariah had to keep on asking the angel to explain the meaning of the vision. How often do we ask God about things we do not understand? How foolish it is to fret, fume and puzzle over things when, so often, God is waiting to answer our prayer – if only we will persist with our requests. God sometimes tests our faith and our determination by keeping us waiting for his answer; but he does regard our persistence and answer us when we need it.

Then the angel passed on the word of the Lord to Zerubbabel (4:6). Zerubbabel was the governor of the land, a successor to the last king, to whom he was related. It was he who was in charge of the rebuilding of the temple. At this particular time it would appear that he was feeling very discouraged. There were many difficulties standing in the way of the completion of the temple. How was he ever going to finish the task? Things had really got on top of him.

These difficulties seemed, to Zerubbabel, just like mountains; yet God spoke graciously to his cast-down servant. He told him to stop trying to do God's work in his own strength. Maybe everything seemed to be against him, but God said,

'"**Not by might** [the strength of many combined] **nor by power,** [that of one man], **but by my Spirit," says the Lord Almighty**' (4:6). In other words, it is God's power which will ensure that the building is completed.

Now what about these mountains of difficulty? God says, '**What are you, O mighty mountain? Before Zerubbabel you will become level ground**' (4:6). Foreign world powers had often been described as mountains (Psalm 68:16-17; 76:4-5; Jeremiah 51:25), but these cannot frustrate God's work. Isaiah prophesies,

> 'Every valley shall be raised up,
>   every mountain and hill made low;
> the rough ground shall become level,
>   the rugged places a plain'

> (Isaiah 40:4).

The power of the Holy Spirit

Do you see what God is saying? You do not have to go and fetch the oil for the temple lamps any more; God himself is supplying the power to light them up. The golden oil is flowing straight into the lampstand.

In the same way Zerubbabel does not have to rely on human 'might' or 'power' any more; God is going to complete the task. How will that be done? He says it will be 'by my Spirit' (4:6). The continuous stream of golden oil is a symbol of the constant presence of the Holy Spirit. 'Apart from me you can do nothing' (John 15:5), said Jesus. The Holy Spirit is the power of God, and without the Holy Spirit's aid nothing of any lasting value can be accomplished.

Many churches today are busy faithfully preaching the gospel, yet few people come to faith in Christ. Why is this? Sometimes the teaching is not the pure gospel; sometimes the preaching is not watered by prayer. Sometimes there may be weeks passing by when no unbelievers are present. But sometimes everything has been done according to God's Word, and still unbelievers are content to sit and listen to the gospel and remain unsaved.

How we need to pray for an outpouring of God's Spirit upon his church and its witness today! Remember that he promises to come with power upon his suppliant people.

But God is sovereign, and he works how, when and where he pleases. In speaking of the work of the Holy Spirit Jesus uses the figure of the wind. He says, 'The wind blows wherever it pleases. You hear its sound, but you cannot tell where it comes from or where it is going. So it is with everyone born of the Spirit' (John 3:8).

At the time of writing this, two people in our fellowship have recently given testimonies of salvation. One, some years ago, read a simple gospel booklet, prayed the prayer of commitment at the end of it, and was saved. The other attended our church for over a year. She sat through a whole series of sermons on the prophet Zechariah, read John Blanchard's *Right with God* (and many other good books). Prayers of commitment did not help her at all. Somewhat frustratedly she said to me, 'These books all tell me that I must repent and believe, but no one will tell me *how* I can believe!' I could only reply, 'It is only by the power of the Holy Spirit that anyone can come to faith in Christ.' Gradually after that her mind and heart became opened to receive the Lord. Eventually she came to realize that God does exist, that Jesus had died to take away her sin and that she had been born again. It is not by mighty actions or by the power of persuasive words that people are saved and the church is built up, but by the sovereign work of the Holy Spirit.

'Not by might ... but by my Spirit'

Leaders in the church are often weighed down by the responsibilities laid upon them. They feel that they will never complete the work God has given them to do. As a result they become spiritually depressed, until they remember that God says, 'It isn't by might, nor by power, but by my Spirit.'

Churches see the work expected of them as very onerous and impossible. How we need to remember that the Lord has given us the power of his Spirit to work through us in our tasks! He never calls us to any work without empowering us to perform it. No wonder that Paul tells us to keep on being 'filled with the Spirit' (Ephesians 5:18). We cannot draw the strength for daily living from within ourselves, but God promises a continual flow of the Holy Spirit into the lives and hearts of those who are fully consecrated to him and his commands.

However, tubes can get clogged up – perhaps those in the golden lampstand did on occasions. Sin within the church can cause a blockage of the flow of God's Holy Spirit in our fellowships and it must be dealt with completely before God's blessing can begin to flow to his people.

The work of the Holy Spirit is to lead us to God. The effect of the Holy Spirit is to empower his people to work and witness for him. Without being continually filled with the Holy Spirit (like the golden lampstand) we cannot shine for Jesus nor help anyone along the Christian pathway.

15.
The problem of sin

Visions 6 and 7

Please read Zechariah 5:1-11

All of the visions so far have spoken of blessing for God's people. The first three foretold outward prosperity for Israel and Jerusalem. The fourth and fifth tell us of inward blessing as the nation looks unto him whom 'they have pierced' (Zechariah 12:10) and God removes 'the sin of this land in a single day' (Zechariah 3:9).

Now we turn to a darker side. Sin must be dealt with. 1 Peter 4:17 tells us, 'It is time for judgement to begin with the family of God, and if it begins with us, what will the outcome be for those who do not obey the gospel of God?'

We have sinned, and we so often seem insensitive to the awfulness of our wrong-doing. We are little better than Judah of old. This chapter ought to make us consider the problem of our individual sins and the dreadful state of the church today because of their sinful, selfish attitude, actions and failures.

Moral failure

Zechariah had perhaps been thinking about the sins of the land. Judah had been punished for seventy years in the Babylonian captivity. That had been a dreadful time for most of them. They were glad to be free again and back in their own land. Now they were trying to rebuild the ruined temple and re-establish the regular worship of the one true God.

But something was wrong. Sin was still present with them. Zechariah was to preach, urging them to live morally upright lives in the sight of God and before their fellow men. '"These are the things you are to do: Speak the truth to each other, and render true and sound judgement in your courts; do not plot evil against your neighbour, and do not love to swear falsely. I hate all this," declares the Lord' (Zechariah 8:16-17). Obviously these were some of their besetting sins. Another was the love of stealing, particularly in regard to commercial transactions.[1]

In view of their moral failure God now reveals to Zechariah what he plans to do about the individual sins of the Jews (the sixth vision) and the very principle of wickedness itself (the seventh vision).

The sixth vision: the flying scroll (5:1-4)

Zechariah saw something flying through the air. It was a flying scroll (5:1). A scroll was the normal kind of book in those days. It consisted of a very long piece of papyrus which was made up of reeds sewn together. This long sheet of papyrus (or leather) could be rolled up on sticks at each end.

Torah (Law) Scrolls are still precious in Jewish synagogues; everyone stands up when the scrolls are taken out of the ark (a kind of cupboard). When a scroll is read a small portion is exposed at a time. When the reader wishes to move on to the next section of writing the parchment is unrolled from one stick and the slack rolled on to the other one.

But as Zechariah viewed this flying scroll he saw that it was completely unrolled. The reason for this was so that all of the writing on it could be read easily. Like the scroll in Revelation 5:1, it was covered with writing on both sides.

The scroll was very large. A scroll thirty feet long would not be that unusual but one which was fifteen feet wide would be a most surprising phenomenon.

The scroll was flying throughout the whole land. In other words, everyone could see it. You couldn't fail to notice such a large object flying through the air. It was moving about everywhere.

What did the flying scroll signify?

It spoke of the law of God. On one side of it was written: **'Every thief will be banished'** and on the other side: **'Everyone**

who swears falsely will be banished' (5:3). The law given to Moses on Mount Sinai was written on two tables, or tablets, of stone. When Moses came down from the mountain he carried one under each arm. These two tablets of the Testimony were 'inscribed on both sides, front and back' (Exodus 32:15).

Although scholars divide the Ten Commandments in slightly different ways, it is helpful to think of them as two groups of five. The first five commandments signify our duty towards God, and the second five speak of our duty towards our fellow men. If we use that division then the middle commandment of each group is singled out. On one side of the flying scroll was written, 'You shall not steal' (the eighth commandment) and on the other side was written, 'You shall not swear falsely,' Everyone who swears falsely misuses the name of God. The third commandment says, 'You shall not misuse the name of the Lord your God, for the Lord will not hold anyone guiltless who misuses his name' (Exodus 20:4). Thus the middle of each group stood for the whole of the Decalogue.

It is significant also that this scroll was exactly the same size as the Holy Place in the tabernacle (thirty feet by fifteen), and as the porch in Solomon's temple, where various offerings were made upon the altar. The temple was where the presence of God was said to dwell. No one could enter the Most Holy Place, except the high priest on the Day of Atonement. Why was that? Because sin banishes people from the presence of God.

This flying scroll was a symbol of sin, and its curse. The angel said, **'This is the curse that is going out over the whole land'** (5:3). What does Paul say about this curse? 'All who rely on observing the law are under a curse, for it is written, "Cursed is everyone who does not continue to do everything written in the Book of the Law"' (Galatians 3:10). Zechariah 5:4 is one of the most solemn verses in the whole of Scripture: **'The Lord Almighty declares, "I will send it out** [the curse of the law] **and it will enter the house of the thief and the house of him who swears falsely by my name. It will remain in his house and destroy it, both its timbers and its stones.'**

Sin is such a vile thing in the sight of God that he will judge and destroy the sinner and everything connected with him ('the timbers and stones of his house'). God hates sin and says that only death can remove it. But what of those morally upright people who keep most of the law? James says, 'Whoever keeps the whole law and yet stumbles at just one point is *guilty of breaking all of it*' (James 2:10).

Sin, therefore, brings the curse of God upon all those who break the law of God and is 'a cancer that needs to be exorcised from the Body of Christ' (Swaggart).

The vision of the flying scroll speaks, then, of God's judgement upon every unrepentant sinner. No one in 'the whole land' will escape the all-seeing eye of God. The Lord Almighty himself says, 'I will send it [the curse] out' (5:4). This verse is a foretaste of the judgement scene in Revelation 6: 'Then the kings of the earth, the princes, the generals, the rich, the mighty, and every slave and every free man hid in caves and among the rocks of the mountains. They called to the mountains and the rocks, "Fall on us and hide us from the face of him who sits on the throne and from the wrath of the Lamb! For the great day of their wrath has come, and who can stand?"' (Revelation 6:15-17).

The seventh vision: the woman in a basket (5:5-11)

In the vision Zechariah again sees something in the air. This time it is a measuring basket (an ephah) (5:6). This was the kind of basket which came into prominent use during the time of harvest. It was used for measuring the quantity of fruit, vegetables or seed which had been harvested. In this vision, 'It signifies something having come to the full and being ready for judgement; in other words, God has measured Israel's sin and will bring it to judgement.'[2]

This measuring basket had unusual contents. In it sat a woman. She seemed quite content to sit there. She showed no shame when the angel announced, **'This is wickedness'** (5:8). No wonder that wickedness is illustrated by a brazen harlot who lures men into sin without any qualms at all (Proverbs 6:24-29).

Sin is regularly described in feminine terms. Jezebel is a picture of sinfulness in the extreme (both in the stories about Elijah, 1 Kings 17-21, and also in Revelation 2:20). Babylon is called the 'mother of prostitutes' in Revelation 17 and 18, and it was Eve who tempted Adam to eat of the fruit of the tree which was in the middle of the Garden of Eden (Genesis 3). But let us not be too hard on women. Wickedness is a feminine word in Hebrew; perhaps that is why wickedness is pictured as a woman. In any case the wicked one who is to come is called 'the *man* of sin' in 2 Thessalonians 2.

The heavy lid of the basket

As Zechariah looks he sees that the measuring basket has a lid made out of lead. When this lid is raised to show Zechariah the contents, the woman immediately tries to get out. Wickedness does not like being confined and is always quick to run riot wherever it can. But the angel in the vision very quickly slammed the lid shut: **'And he pushed her** [the woman] **back into the basket and pushed the lead cover down over its mouth'** (5:8).

The destination of the basket

What happened to this basket containing wickedness? It was taken away by two other women. But these women cannot symbolize wickedness, otherwise they would have tried to engineer the escape of the occupant. Zechariah saw that they had **'wings like those of a stork'** (5:9). The stork was a migratory bird which was often seen over Judah. When it flew low it was an indication that it was on a short flight, but when it flew high in the air it was a sure sign that its journey was to be a long one. These women flew high, **'they lifted up the basket between heaven and earth'** (5:9). It is interesting to note also that the stork was one of the unclean birds listed in Leviticus (Leviticus 11:19).

These two women had the wind in their wings, to speed them on their way (5:9). They needed this extra power because the journey was important and urgent. There could be no possibility of failure in the mission. Wickedness must be removed from the land as quickly and surely as possible!

The basket, with its evil contents, was taken to Babylon – the land of wickedness. This was where God's people had suffered for almost seventy years and this was where wickedness belonged. A house was going to be built for its habitation, and **'the basket will be set there in its place'** (5:11). This signifies permanent banishment. The word 'set', to our ears, indicates a permanent fixing – as something which is 'set' in cement.

Sin must be removed from God's presence

Babylon was the original place of idolatry. It was there, in the land of Shinar, that the proud inhabitants tried to build a tower to reach up to God (Genesis 11). It is to this same place that, symbolically, wickedness will be banished. The name that Jesus used for everlasting punishment and destruction was hell.

Many today are living lives of idolatry. They do not fear God; they only seek to build a city for themselves 'with a tower that reaches to the heavens, so that [they] may make a name for [themselves]' (Genesis 11:4). They worship the gods of riches, power, popularity and luxury. They do not consider where their eventual destiny will be. Will it be Babylon or the new Jerusalem? Will it be with the devil and his evil hosts or will it be with Christ? Will it be in hell or in heaven?

They do not realize that their sin problem will have to be dealt with one day. They do not know that their sins are keeping them from God right now and, if they are not cleansed, will banish them for ever from his sight when they die. The wonder of the gospel message is that there is an answer to the problem of sin. Christ has died on the cross to take away the sins of his people and to deal with the very principle of wickedness itself. Oh that God's people would be more diligent in warning the unconverted of the punishment that awaits those who die in their sin! God says to his servants, 'When I say to the wicked, "O wicked man, you will surely die," and you do not speak out to dissuade him from his ways, that wicked man will die for his sin, and *I will hold you accountable for his blood*' (Ezekiel 33:8).

All sin is repugnant in the sight of God. He has designed his land and his city to be holy. That means that it will be pure and free from sin. In the description of the new Jerusalem in Revelation we read that 'Nothing impure will ever enter it, nor will anyone who does what is shameful or deceitful'

(Revelation 21:27). 'No longer will there be any curse' in it, either (Revelation 22:3). It is God's design that, one day, we shall all be free from sin and the very principle of wickedness itself. But that will not happen on this side of the grave.

> Dear dying Lamb, thy precious blood
>   Shall never lose its power,
> Till all the ransomed church of God
>   Be saved, *to sin no more.*
>
> (William Cowper).

God deals severely with sin. His curse, the law, enters the house of every sinner in the world and one day, at the Judgement, they will all be punished for their lawlessness. 'The soul who sins is the one who will die' (Ezekiel 18:4) and everything that he owns will be destroyed and rendered valueless. The good news is that another has taken away the curse of the law: 'Christ redeemed us from the curse of the law by becoming a curse for us, for it is written: "Cursed is everyone who is hung on a tree"' (Galatians 3:13).

16.
The Lord's reign

Please read Zechariah 6:1-15

We now come to the last vision and it may well be that the reader is growing weary of them and is wondering where they will all lead. The Western mind is not used to thinking in pictures like these. That is why parts of the prophecy of Daniel and the book of Revelation are somewhat difficult to understand. Stuart Briscoe says, 'As we do not think in apocalyptic terms, we find the visions strange and unsettling, or just plain boring.'[1]

The eighth vision: the four chariots (6:1-8)

We have now come full circle. The eight visions were all revealed in one night, which corresponds to 15 February 519 B.C. (but remember that the Jewish day began as night-time descended, that is, in the early evening, and ended when it next became dark, that is, the next evening).

This had been some night for Zechariah! It had started and ended with horses, a symbol of swiftness and strength. God had been revealing encouraging truths to his servant Zechariah, and he now had ample material for his preaching to the inhabitants of Jerusalem and the surrounding district. Zechariah could, with confidence, tell the people not to be worried about their enemies. His preaching would be along these lines: 'God is going to overthrow those who oppose you. He is going to finish his work of rebuilding Jerusalem, far beyond anything you can envisage. He is going to cleanse his people and work through them, bringing from them a Messiah who will take away all their sin in a single day. He is not going to do this through armies, or human ingenuity, but through his people who will recognize the power of his Spirit at work in them.'

If we are going to understand the meaning of these visions for God's people today we must try to 'get inside' the situation in Jerusalem in the period 520-518 B.C. and realize what the visions meant to the Jews of Zechariah's day. They were not just given to stimulate the intellect or to provide material for lectures regarding future events. They were revealed to Zechariah so that he could urge the Jewish people to press on with the work of rebuilding the temple and restoring the true worship of God on a regular basis.

The four chariots

'I looked up again', Zechariah said (6:1). This time he saw **'four chariots coming out from between two mountains – mountains of bronze'**. Each of these chariots was drawn by a group of horses. Notice that there is no mention of riders this time (as there was in the first vision). The horses most certainly had riders but what we need to focus our attention on this time is the chariots.

These four chariots remind us of the four groups of horses in the first vision (1:7-11). However, some of the colours of the horses are different this time, and certainly the purpose of the vision is not the same. In the first vision the emphasis is upon the riders who reported to the angel of the Lord on the state of the whole earth. Here, in chapter 6, the purpose of the vision is to show what God is going to do to all the nations of the world.

These four chariots also remind us of the four horsemen of the Apocalypse (Revelation 6:1-7). Those four horsemen rode animals of similar colours to those of Zechariah's eighth vision. Their task is to ride throughout the earth in judgement. The rider of the white horse is to conquer in the name of the Lord (v.2). The rider of the red horse is to cause war (v.4). The rider on the black horse is to bring justice and judgement (vv.5-6), and the rider on the pale horse is 'to kill by sword, famine and plague, and by the wild beasts of the earth' (v.8).

It seems that the main purpose of the different colours of the horses is so that they can be distinguished from each other, but in a general sense red seems to indicate bloodshed, warfare and carnage; white speaks of victory; black is the symbol of grief and death, and dappled represents pestilences of various kinds.

Some will be interested to note that there were *four* chariots. Moore tells us that 'The number four has the same significance here as in the four winds of Daniel (Daniel 7:2), the four cherubs of Ezekiel (Ezekiel 10:4), the four angels at the four corners of the earth in the Apocalypse (Revelation 7:1), and the four horns and the four artificers in the second vision. Alluding to the four points of the compass, it is the symbol of universality, a judgement that goes out in every direction'[2]

The two mountains

These have given rise to great speculation. Some say they were actual mountains surrounding Jerusalem and others that they were spiritual symbols of the immovable foundation of God's promises and purposes. We do know that they were the guardians of the **'presence of the Lord of the whole world'** (6:5). Mountains speak of strength, and so does bronze. It is a powerful alloy and its strength is symbolized in Jeremiah 1:18-19 where the Lord says to Jeremiah, '"Today I have made you a fortified city, an iron pillar and a bronze wall to stand against the whole land – against the kings of Judah, its officials, its priests and the people of the land. They will fight against you but will not overcome you, for I am with you and will rescue you," declares the Lord.'

Perhaps, as Zechariah received this last vision, the morning was coming and the prophet looked up and saw the first rays of the sun glinting on Mount Zion and the Mount of Olives, and they seemed to him like burning bronze. Perhaps he was standing before the temple and saw the bronze pillars which stood on either side of the entrance 'and they grew in the vision to the fabulous size of mountains, guarding the presence of God'.[3]

Whatever these mountains signify, it is what came out from between them which catches our attention.

The four spirits of heaven

Chariots are symbols of war and also of pomp and stately grandeur. In this vision they are not just on show, they mean business! Verse 7 tells us that the powerful horses, which pulled them, were **'straining to go throughout the earth'**. (They were just like God's servants who are eager to do his bidding.)

Zechariah asked his interpreting angel, **'What are these, my lord?** (6:4). The angel told him that they were **'the four spirits of heaven, going out from standing in the presence of the Lord of the whole world'** (6:5). The figure now changes, maybe because chariots cannot be conceived of as moving quickly enough to speed throughout the whole earth. Even these strong animals would get tired after many miles of galloping.

Psalm 104:3-4 speaks of the Lord God is these terms:

> 'He makes his clouds his chariot
>   and rides on the wings of the wind.
> He makes his winds his messengers,
>   flames of fire his servants.'

When we remember that the Hebrew word for 'wind' and 'Spirit' is the same, then we can see how the strong air movements can represent God and the wind, his messengers. Those who were living in the south-eastern parts of Britain on the night of 15 October 1987 can certainly believe that the strong winds are pictures of God moving throughout the world in judgement!

The powerful horses were straining like the wind, and the Lord eventually said, **'Go throughout the earth!'** and they obeyed (6:7). We have a similar picture in Revelation 7:1, where four angels are seen standing at the four corners of the earth, 'holding back the four winds of the earth to prevent any wind from blowing on the land or on the sea or on any tree.

The mission of the four chariots

The horses and chariots went out in different directions, just as the wind comes from all four quarters of the earth. The one with the black horses went towards the north country. This is the direction that anyone would need to go from Jerusalem in order to travel to Babylon. (To go directly north-east would mean travelling across large tracts of arid desert land.)

According to the NIV footnote the one with the white horses followed the black one. Babylon was a powerful enemy which was ripe for a double dose of judgement, because of the way in which they had treated those whom they had captured from the southern kingdom. God had spoken about cruel Babylon and had told his servant Isaiah what he would, one day, do to them:

> 'The Lord has broken the rod of the wicked,
>   the sceptre of the rulers,
> which in anger struck down peoples
>   with unceasing blows,
> and in fury subdued nations
>   with relentless aggression'
>
> (Isaiah 14:5-6).

But it may be that the text of the NIV is correct in saying that the one with the white horses went towards the west (6:6). If this was the case then the enemy in the west would have been the Philistines.

The chariot with the dappled horses was sent to the south. This is the direction anyone would need to take to bring judgement upon Egypt, the traditional enemy of Israel. The meaning of **'dappled'** is uncertain but it carries the idea of 'strong'. Perhaps it can be linked with the pale horse in Revelation 6:7-8 and it symbolizes death to all the enemies of God and his people.

But there is a problem. There is no mention of the east or the chariot with the red horses. Presumably no chariot was despatched to the east because none of Israel's enemies ever attacked them from that direction. As for the chariot with the red horses, we are not told what happened to it. Perhaps it needed to be kept in reserve. God must show his people that he is always prepared. As we would say, God will not be caught 'napping'. He is always ready to 'maintain the honour of his word'.[4]

The outcome of God's judgement

At the end of this last vision the Lord God himself speaks to Zechariah: **'Look, those going towards the north country have given my Spirit rest in the land of the north'** (6:8). God means that his purposes have been accomplished. 'Babylon had dealt so cruelly with Israel in bringing about the latter's captivity that Babylon herself incurred God's wrath and God's Spirit could have no rest till it had vented its displeasure on the offender.'[5]

The crowning of Joshua (6:9-15)

We now come to a symbolic prophetic act. This is a kind of appendix to the visions. It sums up the meaning of them all. The crowning of Joshua was no vision; it actually happened. Zechariah did not 'see' anything this time as he had in the visions, and there is no interpreting angel to explain the meaning of what was happening. Unlike the visions, God now commands Zechariah to go and do something. The prophet says, **'The word of the Lord came to me'** (6:9). He was instructed to go to the house of Josiah son of Zephaniah, who was living in a house in Jerusalem. There he was to meet three people, who it seems, had just returned from exile in Babylon. (Remember that the Jews did not all return at one time; there were many groups coming back to their homeland over a considerable period of time. We can learn of this by studying the opening chapter of Ezra.)

Heldai, Tobijah and Jedaiah had brought gifts back from Babylon and these were to be used in connection with the rebuilding of the temple (see Ezra 6:5). Zechariah was bidden to waste no time, but to go that same day and make a crown from the gold and silver that these Jews had brought with them (6:10-11). This crown was to be a single crown, not a triple one, but was probably made from various circlets of the precious metals. He was then to crown Joshua, the high priest, in the house of Josiah, not in the temple. Then the crown was to be deposited in the temple as a memorial to these three returned exiles and the 'favour' that Josiah showed them by graciously lodging these men as his guests.

The crowning of Joshua was a symbolic act

How do we know this? We know it because it is not recorded
that Joshua the high priest ever reigned over his people; and
we also know this is symbolic because of the words of the Lord
which follow in verses 12-15.

Liberal scholars say that there is a corruption of the text
here and that the name 'Zerubbabel' should be inserted
instead of 'Joshua'. They reason that Zerubbabel came from
the royal line and, therefore, it is much more likely that it is
he who was crowned and who would **'sit and rule on his
throne'** (6:13). Yet we know from the historical record that
there is no mention of Zerubbabel reigning as King of Judah.
Indeed the last mention of him is in Zechariah 4:10. In any
case the Persians would have seen it as a revolutionary act if
the one whom they had appointed as Governor of Judah, to
look after their interests, had allowed himself to be crowned
king of the land.

It is certain that it is Joshua who was crowned. At the half-
way point of the visions – the fourth vision – Joshua is spoken
of, and now he comes on the scene again at the end of the last
vision. Zerubbabel, the governor, and Joshua, the high
priest, had been used much in organizing the people to
rebuild the temple (see Haggai 1:13-15). They were both
important to the work of the Lord. Zerubbabel was
descended from the royal line of King David and Joshua came
from the priestly tribe of Levi. By Zechariah's time any
Jewish king had to come from the royal line of David. And no
priest could be appointed from any other tribe than that of
Levi.

The man whose name is the Branch

It is obvious then that the crowning of Joshua was symbolic of
the crowning of someone who was to come. That is a further
reason why the crown, which was made by Zechariah, was
placed in the temple – to remind the people that there was a
king coming to them who will one day be crowned and who
'will be clothed with majesty and will sit and rule on his throne'
(6:13).

When Zechariah performed the coronation he was to say to

Joshua, **'This is what the Lord Almighty says: "Here is the man whose name is the Branch, and he will branch out from his place and build the temple of the Lord"'** (6:12). Notice the announcement: *'Ecce Homo',* 'Behold the man.' That is what Pilate said to the crowds outside his palace when he introduced the prisoner, Jesus of Nazareth (John 19:5AV).

The Branch was one of the names for the Messiah. It is the name of the servant whom God told Joshua about in Zechariah 3:8. [6] This points unmistakably to the Lord Jesus Christ. He had obscure origins. He was a humble carpenter's son for thirty years. 'He grew up...like a tender shoot, and like a root out of dry ground... He was despised and rejected by men' (Isaiah 53:2-3). And his church too, began as a little flock. True Christians are still in the minority in the world. But the point to notice is the 'branching out'. There is steady and certain growth taking place. One day God's people who, at the beginning, were like 'a mustard seed, which is the smallest seed you plant in the ground...grows and becomes the largest of all garden plants, with such big branches that the birds of the air can perch in its shade' (Mark 4:31-32).

He will build the temple

Twice it is said that the one called 'the Branch' will build the temple (6:12,13). The second time the use is very emphatic. It recalls to our minds the words of Jesus: 'I will build my church and the gates of Hades will not overcome it' (Matthew 16:18). The temple referred to in Haggai and Zechariah is the blood-bought company of the Lord's people – the church, which is still being built with Christ Jesus (the Messiah) himself as 'the chief cornerstone' (Ephesians 2:20).

The Branch will be clothed with majesty. This means 'the kingly glory that shall be his, in spite of his lowly origins'.[7] He will sit and rule on his throne. This speaks of something which is established and sure.

King and priest

No Israelite priest could be a king. So how can the prophecy be fulfilled? The Lord goes on to say, **'There will be harmony between the two'** (6:13). Can two different men consistently reign without ever falling out? This can only work efficiently if both offices are combined in one person. We saw the same idea when we examined the two olive trees in Zechariah 4. Now we have the same concept. The only one who can fulfil both functions is foretold in Psalm 110:4: 'You are a priest for ever, in the order of Melchizedek.' Yes. It is the Lord Jesus Christ who sits as a **'priest on his throne'** (6:13). He is the kingly-priest and the priestly-king (see Hebrews 7:11- 28).

For Jews only?

There is one more wonderful thing to notice: **'Those who are far away will come and build the temple of the Lord'** (6:15). Here is good news again. This temple is not just for Jews but for Gentiles as well, and they will help in the building up of 'the temple'.

Now stop for a moment and try to place yourself in the position of these returned exiles. They had had enough of the Gentiles. They had suffered at their hands and they were now thrilled to be a nation of pure Jews again. They had rebuffed the offer of help from the people who were already in the land (Ezra 4:3) and they were going to do all they could to maintain their separateness. The temple was too holy to allow people from other races to help with its construction. Whatever then, does Zechariah mean by saying, 'Many nations will be joined with the Lord in that day and will become my people'? (2:11). And why will **'those who are far away'** come and build the temple of the Lord?

The eleven who received the Great Commission from Jesus himself must also have been puzzled, for similar reasons, when he instructed them to 'go and make disciples *of all nations,* baptizing them in the name of the Father and of the Son and of the Holy Spirit' (Matthew 28:19). 'In the Jewish context, these "nations" are the "outsiders" – tribes and peoples at a distance from the social and religious life of Israel. They are the people who are "far away"...They are also the "enemies", a political, military, and religious threat to the integrity of Israel.'[8]

It is no wonder that Jonah was appalled at God's call for him to go to heathen Nineveh and preach repentance to its people. How then, can proud Judah and the heathen nations ever be brought together? Paul tells us the answer: 'But now in Christ Jesus you who once were far away have been brought near through the blood of Christ. For he himself is our peace, who has made [Jew and Gentile] one and has destroyed the barrier, the dividing wall of hostility' (Ephesians 2:13-14). In the church of the redeemed, the true temple, the Jews will welcome the Gentiles who have been washed from their sins in the precious blood of Christ and together they will work for the building up of the church.

It is the duty and privilege of God's people today to go out and preach the gospel in their own and other lands. We have the command from the Lord himself to do this. We have the motivation; the Lord says, 'Those who are far away *will* come.' And we have the promise of God's power: '"Not by might nor by power, but by my Spirit," says the Lord Almighty' (4:6).

Our King has been crowned

God has numberless hosts of angels to protect his own people. Just as Satan is 'roaming through the earth and going to and fro in it' (Job 1:7), so God is busy on behalf of his people. The devil does his worst throughout the world in causing the persecution of the saints, but it is the joy of Christian believers to know the presence of Christ in all their afflictions. The people of God in the days in which the Revelation was written were undergoing many trials and so the Lord gave them the last book in the Bible to be a comfort and strength to their faith. We need to remember that the Lord Almighty will have the final word and perform the last action, and those who trust in him will be kept safe from all real harm and danger.

Jesus has been crowned King of the Universe. Some say that the day of his ascension was his coronation day. The Lord Jesus Christ is now reigning and ruling in heaven as our great high-priestly King. The book of the Revelation has many instances of the kingship of Christ. John saw a great multitude standing before the throne and in front of the Lamb saying, 'Salvation belongs to our God, who sits on the throne and to the Lamb' (Revelation 7:10). Loud voices cried from heaven, 'The kingdom of the world has become the kingdom of our

Lord and of his Christ, and he will reign for ever and ever'
(Revelation 11:15). And those who had been victorious sang,

> 'Great and marvellous are your deeds,
>   Lord God Almighty.
> Just and true are your ways,
>   King of the ages.
> Who will not fear you, O Lord,
>   and bring glory to your name?
> For you alone are holy.
> All nations will come
>   and worship before you,
> for your righteous acts have been revealed'
> (Revelation 15:3-4).

The kingly rule of Christ is an oft-repeated fact throughout
the New Testament.

Jesus as King requires his subjects to be loyal and faithful to
him. How loyal are we to Christ? How faithful to his commands are we? We cannot say Jesus is our King unless we own
his allegiance, unless we follow him and honour him in everything that we do. Jenny Mussey gives us some advice on this
subject.

> King of my life, I crown thee now,
> Thine shall the glory be;
> Lest I forget thy thorn-crowned brow,
> Lead me to Calvary.
>
> Lest I forget Gethsemane,
> Lest I forget thine agony,
> Lest I forget thy love for me,
> Lead me to Calvary.

17.
A question of fasting

Please read Zechariah 7:1 – 8:23

Almost two years had passed since the prophet Zechariah had
received the eight visions that God had given him to encourage the Jews to press on with the work of the Lord. We have
now reached the night of 7 December 518 B.C. (i.e. the
fourth day of the ninth month of the fourth year of the reign
of King Darius in Babylon, 7:1). The work of the temple was
going ahead with reasonable speed and efficiency. There
seem to have been no more interruptions to it and from Ezra
6:13-15 we learn that the building was completed two years
later.

Everything seemed to be proceeding smoothly for the
inhabitants of Judah, and they were anticipating a more
peaceful life. Since they had resumed work on the temple
their enemies appear to have left them alone and the problems of the poor harvests (Haggai 1:6) seem to have
diminished. Religion was getting back to normal as well. At
this point a delegation of men came to Jerusalem to seek the
Lord regarding a certain problem.

Chapters 7 and 8 form a kind of interlude between the two
halves of the book. The call to repentance and the eight
visions, with their enacted appendix (6:9-15), form the first
half of Zechariah, and the oracles and prophecies regarding
the Messiah and his kingdom largely occupy chapters 9-14.
The question brought by the men of Bethel takes up the two
middle chapters of the book.

The problem of fasting

The people of Bethel (a town some ten miles north of

Jerusalem) sent a delegation to entreat the Lord about the advisability of continuing with religious fasts.

The old name for Bethel was Luz (Genesis 28:19). It was a place of religious worship. In fact Jeroboam I had erected a golden calf there at one time to save the inhabitants of the town the trouble and effort of travelling to Jerusalem to worship God. Naturally this had led to the sin of idolatry, and people even travelled as far as Dan to worship at the feet of a twin golden calf which had also been set up there (1 Kings 12:28-30). The people had forgotten what God had taught them at the foot of Mount Sinai when Aaron built a golden calf for the people to worship (Exodus 32). 'Bethel had developed its own religious ritual and had its own sanctuary and priests. Bethel was a symbol of schism and idolatry and of a divided nation.'[1]

However, following the punishment of the Assyrian exile it seems that the people of Bethel had now learnt their lesson and, on the face of it anyway, were wanting to show their submission to the Jerusalem temple. They did this by sending two of their important citizens, **'Sharezer and Regan-Melech, together with their men, to entreat the Lord by asking the priests of the house of the Lord Almighty and the prophets, "Should I mourn and fast in the fifth month, as I have done for so many years?"'** (7:3).

These men came with a religious question and they went to religious people for an answer. They asked the priests of the temple because it was their duty to give decisions on points of the law (Deuteronomy 17:9). They also sought help from the prophets (i.e. Haggai and Zechariah).

When did they observe fast days?

The question they asked concerned a fast in the fifth month. They had been holding this for the past seventy years, together with a fast in the seventh month (7:5). In fact, from 8:19 we see that they also fasted in the fourth month and on the tenth month. Why did they do this?

In the fourth month they fasted to lament the breach in the walls of Jerusalem made by the invading army of Nebuchadnezzar (2 Kings 25:8-10; Jeremiah 52:12-14).

In the fifth month they fasted to commemorate the burning

of the temple and other important buildings (2 Kings 25:8-10; Jeremiah 52:12-14).

In the seventh month they fasted to mark the anniversary of the assassination of Gedaliah, the Governor of Jerusalem (2 Kings 25:22-25; Jeremiah 41:1-3).

On the tenth month they fasted to mourn the beginning of Nebuchadnezzar's siege of Jerusalem (2 Kings 25:1; Jeremiah 39:1; Ezekiel 24:1-2).

The important thing to notice about Jewish fast days is that God only commanded one day as a fast day and that was the Day of Atonement (Leviticus 16:29). Even today a fairly nominal Jew will not fail to spend at least part of the Day of Atonement in the synagogue following the solemn ritual of this day of repentance. None of these other four days was commanded in Scripture.

The people of Bethel were now asking, 'Is there any point in continuing with these fasts now that life in the land is getting back to normal?' They had done so much weeping and mourning that they desired to know whether they could be excused from further fasting. They had been doing their duty (as they saw it); now could they please 'have a break'?

God answered them in two ways. The remainder of chapter 7 gives a negative answer to the question of fasting and chapter 8 gives a positive reply.

The negative answer

In answer to their enquiry, God, through Zechariah, asked a pointed question – not just to the men of Bethel, but to all the people of the land, *and the priests.* He enquired, **'Was it really for me that you fasted? And when you were eating and drinking, were you not just feasting for yourselves?'** (7:5-6). In fact he says that the earlier prophets had asked them the same question, before they were taken away captive to Babylon (7:7).

What God was saying to them, in effect, was 'You have been fasting for the wrong reason. You have been engaging in these mournful religious ceremonies because you are distressed about the destruction that has come upon the land.

You have been doing this because you have had to suffer exile
in Babylon. You have been doing this because you want me to
think well of you. You have been doing this for every reason
apart from the real reason for fasting.'

What is the only genuine reason for believers to fast? It is
to show deep distress about their own sinful ways and a desire
for God to hear their cry and forgive them. It is only then that
blessing will come upon them.

The need for righteous living

God spoke to them again in verse 8. He said, 'You are trying
to please me by performing religious ceremonial, but you are
not behaving correctly.' **'This is what the Lord Almighty says:
"Administer true justice; show mercy and compassion to one
another"'** (7:9). True justice is that which is exercised with
utter impartiality (Ezekiel 18:8). 'Love and compassion' were
advocated by Hosea (Hosea 2:19-21). Orelli says that the 'two
great demands of righteousness and love were made upon the
people constantly by the old prophets'.[2] To show mercy and
compassion *to one another* is certainly an injunction to which
evangelical Christians ought to pay intense heed in these days
when vitriolic exchanges sometimes occur.

Verse 10 speaks of four classes of people who have no one
to care for them. God's people are exhorted not to **'oppress
the widow or the fatherless, the alien or the poor'.** The 'widow
and the fatherless' had lost their breadwinner and defender.
They were in a weak position financially and socially and were
a prey to the unscrupulous (Micah 2:9). The 'alien' was at a
disadvantage simply because he was a stranger and therefore
'different'. And the 'poor' had no bargaining power and were
at the mercy of the rich (Amos 4:1).

In their hearts they were not to **'think evil of each other'.** In
8:17 the almost identical Hebrew is translated **'plot evil
against your neighbour'**, which is probably the sense here as
well.

God was demanding nothing new

The prophets of old had called upon God's people to live like
this:

'He has showed you, O man, what is good.
  And what does the Lord require of you?
To act justly and to love mercy
  and to walk humbly with your God'

(Micah 6:8).

But their forefathers had 'refused to pay attention; stub-
bornly they turned their backs and stopped up their ears'
(7:11). God had said that they were always 'stiff-necked
people' (Deuteronomy 9:6,13,27). They would not even turn
their heads to listen to what God was saying to them (they
behaved as if they had stiff necks!). **They made their hearts as
hard as flint and would not listen to the law or the words that
the Lord Almighty had sent by his Spirit through the earlier
prophets. So the Lord Almighty was very angry'** (7:12). The
Law and the Prophets were the two divisions of the Word of
God in the Old Testament and God's people deliberately
refused to listen to them.

How did God show his anger? He gave them some of their
own medicine. '"When I called, they did not listen; so when
they called, I would not listen," says the Lord Almighty'
(7:13). Notice the irony of God's words. Jamieson, Fausset
and Brown comment at this point: 'Hard hearts must expect
hard treatment. The harder the stone, the harder the blow of
the hammer to break it.'[3]

As a result of the Jews' disobedience to his commands, God
punished them with the captivity in Babylon and other places.
**'I scattered them with a whirlwind among all the nations,
where they were strangers. The land was left so desolate
behind them that no one could come or go. This is how** [God's
people] **made the land desolate'** (7:14).

The motive for religious ceremonies

In reminding them of the past, God was really asking the
people, 'What is the motive behind all your fasting?' If they
were really sorry then they would obey God and care for each
other.

Listen to Amos 5:21-24:

> 'I hate, I despise your religious feasts;
>   I cannot stand your assemblies
> Even though you bring me burnt offerings and grain
>   offerings,
>   I will not accept them.
> Though you bring choice fellowship offerings,
>   I will have no regard for them.
> Away with the noise of your songs!
>   I will not listen to the music of your harps.
> But let justice roll on like a river,
>   righteousness like a never-failing stream!'

In other words, unless God's people show, by their actions, that they are truly sorry for their sins, then God will not accept any outward display of repentance. Robert Hawker says, 'The people were willing to submit to anything [except] real godliness.'[4]

The positive answer

In chapter 8 God gives ten promises of future blessing. Each one begins with, **'This is what the Lord Almighty says ...'** (8:2,3,4,6,7,9,14,18,20,23).

The Lord begins by saying, **'I am very jealous for Zion; I am burning with jealousy for her'** (8:2). He had said the same thing in 1:14. He means by this that he loves his people with a deep love and he wants them to love him in return. He is like a grieving husband who has been deserted by his wife. An increasing number of Christians know the agony which comes when, first of all, they are deserted and then, to make matters worse, they discover that they have been rejected in favour of someone else.

When the people turned away from the one true and living God to worship gods which were false idols, God's heart was heavy with sorrow. But despite all of this, listen to what he says in verse 3: **'This is what the Lord says: "I will return to Zion and dwell in Jerusalem. Then Jerusalem will be called the City of Truth, and the mountain of the Lord Almighty will be called the Holy Mountain."'**

What is the city?

God was speaking of a time in the future when he would return in a remarkable and public way. I believe these verses refer to the new Jerusalem, the heavenly Jerusalem (Galatians 4:25-26; Hebrews 12:22; Revelation 21). Many interpret these verses literally and say that with the establishment of the nation of Israel in 1948 these promises began to come to pass, but I believe that the blessings promised to Israel of old have been transferred to the new Israel, 'God's elect...who have been chosen according to the foreknowledge of God the Father, through the sanctifying work of the Spirit, for obedience to Jesus Christ and sprinkling by his blood' (1 Peter 1:2). These people are now called God's 'chosen people' (1 Peter 2:9).[5]

Edmund P. Clowney writes, 'In the Old Testament the centre for God's praise was Mount Zion...In the New Testament Jesus brings the fulfilment of that picture. No longer is Jerusalem the centre for worship, for Christ is the true temple... We now come in worship to the heavenly Zion where Jesus is. Because heaven is now the centre of our worship, there can be no earthly sanctuary.'[6] Later he says, 'The author of Hebrews warns us that we have not here an abiding city but seek after that which is to come. We are pilgrims, journeying towards the city of God. That city has foundations, and it will endure. But until that city comes to us, we can never give devotion to any city.'[7]

The blessings to come

God says that in the future **'Jerusalem will be called the City of Truth.'** Truth had not always been the hallmark of God's people but when Messiah comes in great power, then the new Jerusalem will be known as the place of truth. Jesus said, 'I am the way and *the truth* and the life. No one comes to the Father except through me' (John 14:6).

'And the mountain of the Lord Almighty will be called the Holy Mountain.' The place of the Lord's presence will be different (holy) from the literal Zion. It had been a heap of rubble. It will be a temple of the Lord – God's dwelling-place once more. Evil will be banished. There will be no sin in that place, for the holy mountain is none other than heaven itself. This is reserved for all of those who know the Lord and seek to honour him in sincerity and truth.

A picture of heaven

In verses 4 and 5 we have a lovely description of heaven: Jerusalem will be inhabited again and be a city of peace. '**This is what the Lord Almighty says: "Once again men and women of ripe old age will sit in the streets of Jerusalem, each with cane in hand because of his age. The city streets will be filled with boys and girls playing there."'**

Old men and women had been taken into captivity but few elderly people had returned from Babylon. They could not face the gruelling three-months walk through the inhospitable lands which lay between Babylon and Judah. However, in the new Jerusalem, which is to come, there will be found 'men and women of ripe old age sitting in the streets' (see Isaiah 65:20). Also boys and girls will play in these same streets (see Isaiah 11:6-9). This all speaks of laughter and joy, without the older ones complaining of the children's noisy play or the younger ones being upset by the presence of the elderly. Notice the relaxed, unhurried atmosphere. There will be time to allow the elderly and the young to refrain from the rigours of labour, for there will be plenty of food and other provisions in the new Jerusalem.

Verse 7 tells us that God will bring back his people from the east and the west. This means that they will come to the heavenly city from all quarters. The sun rises in the east and sets in the west. It covers the whole earth. So God's people will come from all directions '**to live in Jerusalem**' (8:8). He will not just bring them to have a brief stay in the city. They will be God's people and he '**will be faithful and righteous to them as their God**' (8:8). Once again they will be back in covenant relationship with their God (cf. 13:9).

The immediate future

Zechariah then brings his hearers back to the immediate

future (8:9-15). He tells them that things will begin to grow
again. Previously the temple had lain in ruins (Haggai 1:3).
The crops did not grow (Haggai 1:6), and the enemies of
God's people were trying to cause disruption (Ezra 4:4-24).
But now there is a message of hope and this new life begins
when the people obey the Lord. They had listened to the
prophets and started rebuilding the temple (Haggai 1:12-15).
Zechariah had joined Haggai in urging the people to work.
They obeyed God's word, through the prophets, and good
things began to happen. **'This is what the Lord Almighty says:
"You who now hear these words spoken by the prophets who
were there when the foundation was laid for the house of the
Lord Almighty, let your hands be strong so that the temple
may be built'** (8:9).

When the temple work made progress there was employment once again. **"Before that time there were no wages for
man or beast** [no money to buy food for them]. **No one could
go about his business safely because of his enemy, for I had
turned every man against his neighbour. But now I will not
deal with the remnant of this people as I did in the past,"
declares the Lord Almighty'** (8:10-12).

God promises plenty in the land. **'The seed will grow well,
the vine will yield its fruit, the ground will produce its crops,
and the heavens will drop their dew. I will give all these things
as an inheritance to the remnant of this people'** (8:12). As in
Haggai 2:4 God urges them to be unafraid and strong: **'As you
have been an object of cursing among the nations, O Judah
and Israel, so I will save you, and you will be a blessing. Do not
be afraid, but let your hands be strong'** (8:13).

God next promises them a bright future: **'This is what the
Lord Almighty says: "Just as I had determined to bring disaster upon you and showed no pity when your fathers angered
me," says the Lord Almighty, "so now I have determined to do
good again to Jerusalem and Judah. Do not be afraid'** (8:14-
15). Again comes the call to be courageous and then God's
people will reap a great blessing.

However, the people had to keep their side of the bargain
too. **'These are the things you are to do: Speak the truth to
each other, and render true and sound judgement in your**

courts; do not plot evil against your neighbour, and do not love
to swear falsely. I hate all this," declares the Lord' (8:16-17).

The answer to their question

At long last God gives them the answer to their enquiry about
fasting. He said, 'Your fasting shall be turned into feasting.'
**'The fasts of the fourth, fifth, seventh and tenth months will
become joyful and glad occasions and happy festivals for
Judah. Therefore love truth and peace'** (8:19).

As a result of all this feasting, God says that there will be so
much blessing in Jerusalem that many will want to share in it
(8:20-22).

Following the personal testimony of those who will flock to
Jerusalem (8:21) multitudes will stick closely to God's
people: **'In those days ten men from all languages and nations
will take firm hold of one Jew by the hem of his robe and say,
"Let us go with you, because we have heard that God is with
you"'** (8:23).

Ten men signifies a great number. My father used to say,
'Ten to one things will turn out all right. You just see.'
Zechariah prophesies that great numbers of people will
swarm into Jerusalem; and they will give the reason: 'Because
we have heard that God is with you.'

Ritual or true repentance?

God's people today often engage in religious ritual as a substi-
tute for genuine repentance. Tradition, like the keeping of
these fasts on the fourth, fifth, seventh and tenth months,
occupies much time and energy in church life. It would do
congregations good to ask whether their regular meetings
bring them nearer to God and truly honour the Lord Jesus
Christ.

Some churches seem to take a pride in their days of fasting
and almost boast about the whole nights they spend in prayer.
Surely the Lord is saying to us today, 'When you fast, when
you hold your prayer meetings, when you conduct your deep
Bible studies, pay attention to me and don't try to show how

good you are. If you want me to bless you then get yourselves sorted out. Learn what it is to shed genuine tears of repentance for your individual *and church* sins. Do not stop up your ears but listen to me when I speak through my Word. In all your dealings, whether with Christian people or not, be honourable and just. There is a time of great joy coming. Let your hands be strong and work. Testify that God is in your midst and invite others to your meetings and they will come and be blessed because they have heard that God is with you.'

Churches are good at passing on bad news, sharing problems and asking prayer for the removal of opposition to the gospel. They are not nearly so ready to declare that the Lord God Almighty is with them and making his power known and felt. Today the Lord is calling his people to 'declare his salvation from day to day'.

18.
The righteous king

Please read Zechariah 9:1-17

There have always been enemies opposed to God's people. One of the things that characterize Christians is the fact that they suffer. Jesus himself said, 'In this world you will have trouble. But take heart! I have overcome the world' (John 16:33).

In the time of Zechariah Judah was surrounded by enemies. To the north-east was the land of Syria. To the north lay Phoenicia (modern-day Lebanon) and in the south-west was their traditional enemy of Philistia (roughly where the Gaza Strip is today).

How were God's people going to cope with these enemies? Zechariah tells us in verse 1: **'For the eyes of men and all the tribes...are on the Lord.'** It is always good for people to look to the Lord. When they are troubled or anxious, and they do not know where else to turn, then they can look to the Lord who will protect his people. But how sad it is that God's people so often fail to look to the Lord when they are enjoying prosperity and only turn to him when they are in dire trouble!

A new section of the prophecy

With chapter 9 we enter the last part of the prophecy of Zechariah. This is headed 'an oracle', or burden. The word means 'an utterance from God, usually concerning judgement'. Zechariah 9:1 says, **'The word of the Lord is against the land of Hadrach',** and 12:1 says, **'This is the word of the Lord concerning Israel.'**

Although the Messiah is introduced more clearly in this last half of the book and many blessings are promised to Israel, it would seem that chapters 9-11 deal largely with God's judgements upon the world powers (e.g. Hadrach) and chapters 12-14 with God's judgements upon Israel (which were necessary because of her need to be checked; she was prone to stray into sinful ways).

The present-day parallels are easily seen. God will grant his believing people victory over their enemies. Satan and his evil powers will ultimately be defeated, but the church too is prone to wander and she needs frequent admonitions to make sure that she obeys the Lord.

God's eye is on his people (9:1-8)

200 years after this prophecy was given Alexander the Great was to march through the land on his way to India. Although he did not acknowledge the one true and living God, God was going to use him, like Cyrus before him, to bring about his purposes. The short but effective work of Alexander was going to pave the way for the gospel message some 200 years later. Because of Alexander's conquest of so many countries, Greek culture would become the main influence in the whole Mediterranean area. Greek would be the universal language used by all the educated people in each country, and Alexander would pave the way for the Romans to build their long, straight and safe roads linking the whole empire together. All of these things would contribute to a rapid spread of the gospel in the early Christian era. The New Testament was written in Greek, it was easy for people to move from one country to another because there were no frontiers in the Roman Empire, and the good roads made for rapid communications between towns.

Syria

For a long time critics stated that the name Hadrach was a mistake because history knew of no such place; however, scholars now accept that Hadrach did exist and it stood near to the city of Damascus, the capital of Syria.

Zechariah prophesied that 'The word of the Lord...will rest upon Damascus...and upon Hamath too, which borders on it' (9:1-2). Damascus and its cities were great powers, but God said that his people need not fear because he had his eye on them. They were the 'apple' of his eye (2:8). It mattered not whether the opponents of God's people were great or small; every power rising against God's kingdom would be destroyed. And often the destruction of a heathen power meant deliverance for God's people.

Phoenicia

Tyre and Sidon were noted for their wisdom: **'they are very skilful'** (9:2). For many years they had commanded respect from all the surrounding nations. Tyre especially had grown very wealthy. Because she grew, and needed more land, she moved part of her city to an offshore island: **'Tyre has built herself a stronghold'** (9:3). So strongly was this island protected that it even withstood a thirteen-year siege by Nebuchadnezzar from 605-562 B.C. (read about it in Ezekiel 29:17-18).

The wealth of these cities was legendary: **'She has heaped up silver like dust, and gold like the dirt of the streets'** (9:3). These immense riches came to Tyre through its world-wide commerce. It had one of the few harbours along the eastern shore of the Mediterranean Sea and it was one of the chief centres of trade. It was situated where East and West met and exchanged goods. 'The merchants from these shores worked tin mines in Cornwall and built depots in the Scilly Isles and the Isle of Wight.'[1]

Yet Zechariah prophesied, **'The Lord will take away her possessions and destroy her power on the sea, and she will be consumed by fire'** (9:4). Although Tyre was so strongly defended, nothing would stop Alexander, for the Lord had spoken! Many had tried to capture and destroy her but had failed. Alexander succeeded. How? He besieged her for seven months and during that time he built a causeway (called a 'mole') linking the island to the mainland, which is still there today; he utterly sacked her, killed her chief citizens and deported the rest of the people. Then he completely burnt the city to the ground. And all this was done according to the prophecy which was uttered nearly 200 years before Alexander was born!

Philistia

Tyre had always withstood attacks before, and the cities of the Philistines must have been glad when previous invading armies had been held up by the Phoenicians. However, we can imagine the panic which must have spread throughout the land when proud, wise, rich, powerful Tyre succumbed to the attacks of Alexander. **'Ashkelon will see it and fear; Gaza will writhe in agony, and Ekron too** [the most northerly Philistine town], for her hope will wither' (9:5).

God also said that **'Gaza will lose her king and Ashkelon will be deserted. Foreigners will occupy Ashdod'** (9:5-6). Although Alexander would do all this yet God says, **'I will cut off the pride of the Philistines.'**

Then the Lord turns to the heathen sacrifices performed by the Philistines, who ate raw, or half-raw meat and drank blood – a thing forbidden to Israel as an abomination to the Lord. Through the destruction wrought by Alexander God says, **'I will take the blood from their mouths, the forbidden food from between their teeth'** (9:7).

However, in the midst of all this destruction, even in the land of the Philistines, there will be found a godly remnant: **'Those who are left will belong to our God and become leaders in Judah, and Ekron will be like the Jebusites'** (9:7). These converted Philistines will be greatly honoured; they shall be 'as governors' in Judah. Although the Jebusites initially opposed King David they were eventually incorporated into Israel and amalgamated with God's people. The same thing will happen to godly Philistines.

These people remind us of the Gentiles who joined the early Christian church, the royal priesthood of God. In Acts 8:40 and 9:32-43 we see the fulfilment of this prophecy when Christian congregations became established in former Philistine cities. God always sees the heart and will not destroy those who truly trust in him, whoever they are and whatever they have done.

Jerusalem

But even Alexander's power is not greater than the power of God. Two hundred years before Alexander's conquest Zechariah prophesied that Jerusalem would be saved: **'But I will defend my house against marauding forces. Never again will an oppressor overrun my people, for now I am keeping watch'** (9:8).

For some reason Alexander left the city of Jerusalem and its temple alone. 'When Alexander was advancing upon Jerusalem with great fury, he was arrested by a dream, and induced not only to spare it, but also to confer upon it great privileges.'[2]

This reminds us of Dunkirk. Conditions prevailed whereby thousands of our troops returned across the channel to fight another day. Many people believe that God was behind this and that the Lord wrought a great deliverance for the British people in May 1940. It is certainly true that God will defend his house and protect the honour of his name.

God provides a King for the deliverance of his people (9:9-13)

Zechariah predicted that the Messiah would enter Jerusalem in triumph. The Messiah was the anointed servant of God who would deliver the people from their bondage. The Messiah was the one all the Jews were waiting for; they are still waiting today if they do not recognize the Lord Jesus as God's Christ.

God had often promised a deliverer for his people, one who had been chosen by him to set captives free. The Messiah would defeat all the enemies of Israel. When we think of Jewish history we realize that the Jews have often been in need of deliverance. Many, including Hitler, have tried to stamp them out; and, certainly in the time of Jesus, the Romans were seen as the oppressors of God's people. They were enemies who needed to be cast out.

Christians believe that Jesus of Nazareth is the Messiah, the chosen one of God. They believe that when Jesus rode into Jerusalem on the first 'Palm Sunday' he was declaring to all that he was God's anointed one, and that he had come to bring freedom. Both Matthew and John quote Zechariah 9:9 and say that Jesus fulfilled it when he rode into Jerusalem in triumph and the people shouted 'Hosanna'. They proclaimed that Jesus was the Messiah who had come to bring deliverance for God's people.

A cause for rejoicing

'Rejoice greatly, O Daughter of Zion! Shout, Daughter of Jerusalem! See, your king comes to you, righteous and having salvation, gentle and riding on a donkey, on a colt, the foal of a donkey' (9:9).

The people of Jerusalem were to 'rejoice greatly'. They were to 'shout'. When we are giving good news we want to shout and tell everyone about it. We cannot imagine people using a dreary, boring voice to say, 'My son's been chosen to play for England.' 'I've just heard that my brother is to be made a Knight Commander of the British Empire.' 'My lovely cat has had three beautiful kittens.' Good news is meant to cause excitement. It is to be spread around as quickly as possible.

He is King

'See your king comes to you.' Jesus is King. That means that he is the one who reigns, the one whose rule is over the whole land. This king is described to God's people as 'your king', and he is spoken of as 'coming to you'. Does that not excite you? God's people have a King of their own who is coming *to them*. The Jews had not had a king since 587 B.C.

When the crowds on the way to Jerusalem saw Jesus, they called out, 'Hosanna to the son of David!' (Matthew 21:9). 'Hosanna' means, 'Save now!' or 'God is going to save us.'

Jesus came as king of his people. He reigns to protect and care for his people; and his people should gladly acknowledge his authority and rule over them. Therefore, they should willingly submit to him and say, 'What you say to us we will do.'

He is righteous

Zechariah said, 'Your king is righteous.' That means that he is just in all that he does. He is not like an earthly king who only does what is best for his own advancement in the eyes of his people. This righteous king is 'the Lord our righteousness' (Jeremiah 23:6). He is always fair and honest in all his dealings with mankind. No one can have real cause to complain at the way he administers justice.

He is one 'having salvation'

This does not just mean that he possesses salvation. It means that he dispenses salvation. It is only in God's chosen one that true deliverance can be found. And how can he give salvation? He can grant salvation to an undeserving people because he is just. He places *himself* under the law and takes upon himself the sin of man and its penalty (Isaiah 53:8; John 1:29). Jesus is the only Saviour. No wonder the people are exhorted to 'rejoice greatly' and 'shout'.

He is gentle and humble

This powerful conquering king is now seen, not riding a triumphal war horse, but as one who is **'gentle and riding on a donkey, on a colt, the foal of a donkey'**. Both the ass and her colt were borrowed (Matthew 21:2). Jesus was so lowly and poor that he could not afford to buy his own transport. And he shows his humility by riding a donkey.

This must have puzzled many in the crowd on that first 'Palm Sunday'.

They were expecting the Messiah to come as a conqueror of the Romans. They were looking for God's chosen one to set them free, but this man came, not riding a powerful steed, the symbol of conquest and military power, but riding a donkey, which was mainly used as a simple beast of burden. It was usually thought of as a humble and insignificant animal, although on occasions donkeys had been ridden by kings and judges.

The Messiah's way to victory

The first time Jesus came to this earth he came in humility and peace, but he is going to come again. Then the way of war will be banished: **'I will take away the chariots from Ephraim and the war-horses from Jerusalem, and the battle-bow will be broken'** (9:10).

Jesus said, 'My kingdom is not of this world' (John 18:36). He came as King to rule in the hearts and lives of all those whom he delivers from the bondage of their sin. He came to dwell in people's hearts. He came to bring peace.

Not only will the Jews enjoy the blessings of God's kingly reign but **'He will proclaim peace to the nations. His rule will extend from sea to sea and from the River** [Euphrates] **to the ends of the earth'** (9:10).

> Jesus shall reign where'er the sun
> Doth his successive journeys run:
> His kingdom stretch from shore to shore,
> Till moons shall wax and wane no more.
>
> (Isaac Watts).

The Messiah will come to set prisoners free. God always keeps his promises. It is by the blood of his covenant (his agreement) that people are saved from the guilt and power of their sinful ways (9:11). In extending his kingdom the Messiah will not overlook his covenant people. His covenant was ratified by blood (Exodus 24:5-8) and this foreshadows the atoning blood of Christ's death on the cross which will purchase freedom for the prisoners of sin.

God says, **'I will free your prisoners from the waterless pit. Return to your fortress, O prisoners of hope; even now I announce that I will restore twice as much to you'** (9:11-12).

Remember what the returned exiles were doing at this time. They were rebuilding the temple and they knew that it did not have the grandeur of Solomon's temple. Laetsch says that 'Satan was trying to imprison them in the pit of disappointment, discouragement and unbelief',[3] but the Lord assures them that he is ready to deliver them if only they would return to their fortress (the Rock of Ages, i.e. the Lord Almighty) and have hope (trust) in God; then they would receive the inheritance promised to the first-born (which was a double portion).

The time of the Maccabees

Just as Zechariah was given a prophecy concerning Alexander the Great, so many scholars feel that he was also told to look a little further forward to another event: the rise of the wicked Seleucid ruler Antiochus Epiphanes IV. This evil man tried to destroy the Jewish religion, even offering a pig (an 'unlean' animal) upon the altar in the temple, but under the leadership of Judas Maccabeus, he was deterred from his evil intentions.

Verse 13 shows God using the southern kingdom (Judah) as a bow, together with the northern kingdom (Ephraim) as an arrow, to rouse up the Jews **'like a warrior's sword'** against Greece (both Alexander and Antiochus Epiphanes were Greeks).

Jesus is coming again (9:14-17)

Jesus *is* coming back again a second time as he promised. When he returns the next time he will come with power and great might. **'Then the Lord will appear over them; his arrow will flash like lightning. The Sovereign Lord will sound the trumpet; he will march in the storms of the south, and the Lord Almighty will shield them. They will destroy and overcome with slingstones. They will drink and roar as with wine; they will be like a full bowl used for sprinkling the corners of the altar. The Lord their God will save them on that day as the flock of his people. They will sparkle in his land like jewels in a crown. How attractive and beautiful they will be! Grain will make the young men thrive, and new wine the young women'** (9:14-17).

When Christ comes the second time it will be to bring great judgement upon the earth. God will destroy all his enemies, but great will be the rejoicing of his own blood-bought people.

Listen to what Peter says about the end times: 'The day of the Lord will come like a thief. The heavens will disappear with a roar; the elements will be destroyed by fire, and the earth and everything in it will be laid bare' (2 Peter 3:10).

It will be dreadful **'on that day'**. The enemies of the Lord will be defeated and God's people will be given power to overcome them. They will have strong weapons of destruction in their hands, they will roar like drunkards and dash all around them vast quantities of blood (9:15) which being, as it were, sprinkled on the corner of the altar, will drench two sides of it.

Yet God's people will **'sparkle in his land like jewels in a crown'**. Malachi says, '"They will be mine," says the Lord Almighty, "in the day when I make up my treasured possession"' (Malachi 3:17).

God's promises to his church

These wonderful promises to Israel are made over to the people of God today – the church. God has his eye upon her, yet she foolishly trembles at the approach of the enemy and is fearful at the news of every inroad made by Satan. How God's people ought to have their eyes on the Lord! They may feel threatened. They may feel as though they are prisoners. They may feel powerless to do anything. Yet there is good news! The Lord has come to bring salvation, to proclaim peace, to extend his kingdom, to remind his church of his covenant with them and to make them overcomers against their enemies.

Let us remember that Christ is coming again and that the Lord will 'save us on that day as the flock of his people'. God's people are as precious as 'crown jewels', like diamonds sparkling in the soil. A field of diamonds would be highly valued; so is the church in God's sight. They are 'chosen by God and precious to him' (1 Peter 2:4).

Do these facts not make us want to stir ourselves up and press forward in the work of building up God's kingdom? Remember the 'night is coming, when no one can work' (John 9:4).

19.
God cares for his people

Please read Zechariah 10:1-12

When we sit on our own we so often think that no one cares how we feel. We try our best and endeavour to do what is right, but we get nowhere. It seems as though no one understands our problems and frustrations. Everyone is so busy that they do not have time to listen to us or pay attention to our anxieties and concerns. It seems as though we might just as well not belong to a church for what little notice the pastor takes of us. We think, 'I might as well not bother to put myself out in trying to help others for what thanks I get. Why bother with anything?' And sometimes we get so low that we are tempted to think that not even God cares.

The inhabitants of Jerusalem were probably feeling like that. They had made good progress (at last!) with the rebuilding of the temple but there were still many problems to solve. Where could they go for sound advice? Who would help them as they struggled with their identity crisis? Who cared what they thought anyway?

It is at this point that Zechariah delivered the oracle which began at the start of chapter 9. He said to them, 'Don't be cast down. The Lord will appear for you. "Rejoice greatly, O Daughter of Zion! Shout, Daughter of Jerusalem! See, your king comes to you, righteous and having salvation, gentle and riding on a donkey, on a colt, the foal of a donkey"' (Zechariah 9:9).

He said that the Jews were just like wandering sheep, but God would provide a Shepherd for them. He said to them, **'The Lord Almighty will care for his flock'** (10:3). It was in 9:16 that Zechariah introduced this ancient concept of God's people as sheep in need of a shepherd to care for (pasture) them. Throughout chapter 10 he reiterates the fact that God will care for his sheep. He will do so by being with them. 'Because the Lord is with them, they will fight and overthrow the horsemen' (10:5). God will strengthen them (10:6,12). He will restore them (10:6). He will have compassion on them (10:6). He will call them (10:8). He will gather them (10:8). He will redeem them (10:8). He will bring them back from foreign lands (10:10). And he will provide territory for them (10:10).

To receive these many blessings they must do two things. They must seek help from the correct place, and they must follow the right leadership.

Seek help from the correct place

To receive God's blessing his people must go to the fount of all blessing. They must seek God (10:1). The first word in this chapter is 'ask'. The problem with the whole of Israel was that they often asked in the wrong quarter. If we want to receive something then we must approach the person with the power to bestow it and ask him in an appropriate manner. Zechariah encouraged the Jews to 'ask the Lord'.

Ask God for blessing

When the first temple was completed and Solomon had consecrated it to God's service, the Lord appeared to the king at night and told him how the people could receive his blessing. God implied that bad harvests, caused by lack of rain and plagues of locusts, came about because of the people's wickedness. However, he said that 'If my people, who are called by my name, *will humble themselves* and *pray* and *seek my face* and *turn from their wicked ways,* then I will hear from heaven and will forgive their sin and will heal their land' (2 Chronicles 7:13-14).

One of the problems that had troubled the newly returned exiles (as we have frequently seen) was poor harvests. They needed the former rain, in the autumn, to help the newly sown seed to sprout and grow. Then they needed the latter rain, in the springtime, to enable the ears of corn to swell on their stalks.

Zechariah opens this chapter by reminding the people that when they ask the Lord for what they truly need, he will provide it. After all, God is the provider of all things – including the weather: **'Ask the Lord for rain in the springtime; it is the Lord who makes the storm clouds. He gives showers of rain to men, and plants of the field to everyone'** (10:1). In the same way God will answer his people's prayer for restoration: 'I will restore them because I have compassion on them' (10:6).

To relate this to the needs of the church today we can say that we need 'spiritual rain' to fall upon the seed which we have sown. 'Rain is a symbol of deeper spiritual blessing and God alone can meet those needs.'[1] For spiritual blessing among God's people today there needs to be faithful sowing of spiritual seed, that is, the true teaching of God's Word. This seed should be watered by prayer and faith (expectation of a good harvest), together with the careful weeding out of unhelpful influences. It is the Lord alone who can give a plentiful harvest, and we are foolish if we look to any other source for success in our work.

1. Turn aside from idols

In verse 2 Zechariah highlights some of the bad influences upon God's people. Throughout their existence Israel had regularly turned aside from the one true and living God and had turned towards the gods of the nations around them. In Jeremiah 2:10-11 the Lord takes his people on an imaginary (aerial?) journey. He takes them over the western nations (Kittim) and then over the eastern nations (Kedar) and says,

> 'Observe closely;
> see if there has ever been anything like this:
> Has a nation ever changed its gods?
> (Yet they are no gods at all.)
> But my people have exchanged their Glory
> for worthless idols.'

It is incredible that nations can carry on bowing down to

idols which can never hear or answer prayers. But has anyone ever heard of any nation getting tired of their false gods and abandoning them? No. Yet not only is it patently obvious that these are worthless images, but God's people regularly turned aside from their God, who is the only true God, and worshipped these false idols.

Zechariah bluntly says, **'The idols speak deceit'** (10:2). Idolatry was clearly forbidden in the second commandment: 'You shall not make for yourself an idol in the form of anything...' (Exodus 20:4). The word translated idols here *(teraphim)* is used for the household gods belonging to families. Remember Rachel in Genesis 31:19? When she left her father Laban to travel with her husband Jacob to his home, she stole her household gods. Why? She took them for protection and blessing (rather like the way people wear gold or silver crosses, or St Christophers around their necks today). She wanted something to worship that she could see. But God always condemned their use. He said, 'If you are worshipping them, then you are not worshipping me.' They had to learn that God is a jealous God and that he alone is to be worshipped. We saw that in 1:14 and 8:2.

It is easy for us to laugh at the ridiculous sight of someone bowing down to a god which is the work of man's hands, but we need to stop and ask ourselves if we have greater affection for anything or anyone than we do for the Lord. Idols come in as many forms today as they did in the days of Zechariah. Churches can idolize their pastor or their form of service or their doctrinal slant. If anything has the affection which rightly belongs to God alone, then that idol is preventing the flow of God's blessing to a church or people. William Cowper sums it all up beautifully in his hymn which starts, 'O for a closer walk with God'. One of the verses says,

> The dearest idol I have known,
>   Whate'er that idol be,
> Help me to tear it from thy throne,
>   And worship only thee.

2. Turn aside from diviners

To receive God's blessing his people had also to turn away

from 'diviners'. **'Diviners see visions that lie; they tell dreams that are false'** (10:2).

Wherever there were true prophets, there were also false ones. These false prophets were sometimes called 'diviners'. These were people who predicted the future. We have their counterparts with us today – and they are just as false, and just as popular! Many newspapers have their daily horoscopes and tarot card readers, and ouija board devotees are very active in our society.

To those who read their 'stars' in their women's magazine, television journals or newspapers a word of warning is necessary. You may think it is only just a bit of harmless fun but if you want God's blessing in your life then shun these things. Listen to Jesus: 'Watch out for false prophets. They come to you in sheep's clothing, but inwardly they are ferocious wolves' (Matthew 7:15). If God's people want to receive his blessing in their lives then they must forsake all false prophets. Their idle dreaming will lead them away from God. As God provided true prophets in Bible days, so he provides his Word and faithful expositors of it today.

Follow the right leadership

The people of Judah were wandering astray. They had no shepherd looking after them: **'The people wander like sheep'** (10:2). They were like the Jews in the days of Jesus. Mark tells us that Jesus had compassion on the crowd, 'because they were like sheep without a shepherd' (Mark 6:34). Who was to blame for this sad situation? It was the religious leaders who were at fault. They were not doing the job that God had called them to do. So Zechariah warns those who should have been leading the people in the ways of God. The Lord says, **'My anger burns against the shepherds, and I will punish the leaders'** (10:3). The leaders of Israel were only looking after themselves and keeping the best food for themselves instead of feeding and caring for the sheep of the flock. The whole of Ezekiel 34 refers to the shepherds and the sheep and the first ten verses of that chapter refer specifically to shepherds who were neglecting their charges and keeping the best for themselves. God sums up his complaints about these selfish shepherds by saying, 'I am against the shepherds and will hold them accountable for my flock. I will remove them from tending the flock so that the shepherds can no longer feed themselves. I will rescue my flock from their mouths, and it will no longer be food for them' (Ezekiel 34:10).

The shepherd-king

Ancient kings were called 'shepherds'. Jacob called God 'the Shepherd, the rock of Israel' (Genesis 49:24). David said, 'The Lord is my shepherd' (Psalm 23:1). And Ezekiel spoke of the successor of David as the ideal shepherd: 'I will place over them one shepherd, my servant David, and he will tend them; he will tend them and be their shepherd' (Ezekiel 34:23). This Shepherd-King, to whom Ezekiel refers, is the Messiah of Israel, the Lord Jesus Christ, the only Saviour. Remember that the Hebrew word 'Messiah' is the same as the Greek word 'Christ'. They both mean God's anointed one, his chosen servant, the deliverer.

The Messiah

There is a lovely description of the Messiah in verse 4: **From Judah will come the cornerstone, from him the tent peg, from him the battle-bow, from him every ruler.'** The Messiah, then, will come from Judah. At Christmas time we read the beautiful prophecy: 'But you, Bethlehem Ephrathah, though you are small among the clans of Judah, out of you will come for me one who will be ruler over Israel, whose origins are from of old, from ancient times' (Micah 5:2).

The cornerstone

Out of Judah will come 'the cornerstone'. This building metaphor is often used in Scripture. It was very appropriate for the Jews of Zechariah's time who were busy rebuilding the temple.

If God's people want to build for God's glory then they must build upon a solid and lasting foundation and properly tie in all the parts of the building they are erecting. A cornerstone is what holds all of the building together. It is part of the foundation and therefore supports the whole building and, being placed at the corner of two major walls, it determines the shape and strength of the building. All of the other stones must adjust themselves to this cornerstone. Hendriksen helps us understand the spiritual meaning of Christ being the cornerstone of the church: 'In addition to resting in Christ, the spiritual house is determined as to its character by him. It is he who settles the question as to what this house is to be in the sight of God, and to what is its function in God's universe.'[2]

The tent peg

From Judah will come the Messiah, the tent peg. All those who have been camping will know the importance of having a strong tent peg which has been securely fixed into the ground. The pegs hold the guy ropes taut and these in turn hold up the tent so that it does not collapse. It is interesting to note that the tent pegs which held up the tabernacle in the wilderness were made of bronze (Exodus 27:19).

But some scholars say that the Hebrew word translated 'tent peg' refers to the nail which was driven into the wall on which clothes were hung to keep them neat. In Isaiah 22:23-24 we read of Eliakim, of whom the Lord says he will 'drive him like a peg into a firm place...All the glory of his family will hang on him; its offspring and offshoots – all its lesser vessels, from the bowls to all the jars.'

Whatever the word really means, it certainly speaks of something which is utterly dependable and trustworthy, and which holds everything together. The coming Messiah will be strong, reliable and a unifying force so that God's people will be strengthened in their work and witness for him and his glory.

The battle-bow

This seems to refer back to 9:13, where the Lord says he will 'bend Judah as I bend my bow'. Judah had been small, weak and timid, but God says, 'I will care for this flock and make them like a proud horse in battle' (10:3). Verse 4 apparently is saying that the Messiah will have many different facets to his character. He is not only like 'a Lamb, looking as if it had been slain' (Revelation 5:6), but he is also strong, powerful and fearless in battle, 'the Lion of the tribe of Judah' who 'has triumphed' (Revelation 5:5).

If only Judah will follow the right leader they will gain the victory and will no longer be oppressed. **'Together they will be like mighty men tramping the muddy streets in battle. Because the Lord is with them, they will fight and overthrow the horsemen'** (10:5).

The reuniting of north and south (10:6)

The kingdom had been divided following the death of Solomon. Both parts had been dealt with very severely, the northern kingdom (Israel or Ephraim) being taken into captivity by the Assyrians (from which the vast majority failed to return), and the southern kingdom (Judah) being in exile in Babylon for some seventy years. In speaking of **'the house of Judah'** God is referring to the southern kingdom, and when he mentions **'the house of Joseph'** he means Ephraim (one of Joseph's sons), i.e. the northern kingdom. Zechariah prophesies that God says, **'I will strengthen the house of Judah and save the house of Joseph.'** He is speaking of what he will do to the two halves of the kingdom: the Jews will no longer be weak in the city and countryside around Jerusalem, and at least some of the Israelites of the northern kingdom will return, and both of these separate groups of God's people will be reunited once again. God had heard their cry for help. In the past, he had rejected them, but the day was coming when he would have compassion on them and would restore them to their homeland and bring them again into fellowship with each other, and with himself.

God calls back his people from distant lands (10:7-12)

The remaining verses of this chapter basically concern the

northern kingdom, Ephraim. God says, **'I will signal for them and gather them in'** (10:8). The word 'signal' means 'whistle' and is used of a shepherd calling his sheep. The sheepdog has instructions whistled to it by its master as it drives the sheep into their pen. When God says, **'Surely I will redeem them; they will be as numerous as before'** (10:8), he is using a word which is often used for ransoming from slavery or captivity. He is going to bring his people back and buy them back. He is going to bless them so much that they will multiply in number and be as they were before they were taken away from their land.

Even though the Lord had scattered Israel among many peoples to distant lands **'they and their children will survive, and they will return'**. In their captivity God's people will remember him and, like the children of Israel in Egypt long before, they will call upon him (10:9). Do you recall what the name Zechariah means? It means 'The Lord remembers' (his covenant and his promises). Now God's people will remember him.

Lessons from the past

Centuries earlier the whole of Israel had been slaves in Egypt for some 400 years and, more recently, the northern kingdom had been in captivity in Assyria. God wrought a great salvation for the Israelites when he redeemed them from Egypt (which all Jews remember each spring at Passover time). Likewise God will gather his people from Assyria and bring them back **'to Gilead'** (the northern part of eastern Jordan), **'and there will not be room enough for them'** (10:10).

There will be so many of God's people that the homeland of his church will extend to the ends of the earth (see 9:10). God's people will grow to include all who, through faith in the Saviour of Jews and Gentiles, become the Israel of the New Testament.

'They will pass through the sea of trouble; the surging sea will be subdued and all the depths of the Nile will dry up' (10:11). God's people will pass through many afflictions and troubles. Job said, 'Man is born to trouble as surely as sparks fly upward' (Job 5:7). Jesus told his disciples, 'In this world you will have trouble' (John 16:33), and Paul said, 'We must

go through many hardships to enter the kingdom of God'
(Acts 14:22).

What God did in holding back the Nile (and the Jordan) so
that his people could pass through in safety, he will do again
for his people. He cares for them and leads them through the
seas of troubles when they put their trust in him.

**'Assyria's pride will be brought down and Egypt's sceptre
will pass away'** (10:11). This speaks of those haughty nations
who put great store by their own power and counted God's
people as nothing. The failure of Egypt's power is described
as the loss of her sceptre. 'Two outstanding mighty nations
sink into nothing when they seek to oppose the delivery of
God's people – an everlasting truth concerning all who
oppose the Almighty.'[3]

This chapter ends with the declaration: **'I will strengthen
them in the Lord and in his name they will walk'** (10:12). God
will help his people to go on to complete the tasks he had set
them (rebuilding the temple) and will enable them to keep at
bay all their enemies who would hinder them in the carrying
out of their responsibilities to the Lord. When he says that
they will walk 'in his name' he means that they will live their
lives under his auspices, unlike those who trust in idols or the
power of heathen kings. Speaking of their walk in the Lord
implies that their whole life will be in the strength of and for
the glory of the Lord, and under his leadership. 'The Lord
had not only been a leader in their return, but he would be
their perpetual guardian, and defend them to the end.'[4]

God still calls back his people

God continually calls his people back to himself. He desires
them to seek his face and turn aside from everything which
would claim the love and time which rightly belong to him.
He has provided the only way of redemption, the life, death
and resurrection of the Lord Jesus Christ. When his people
acknowledge their waywardness and return to the Lord he
will receive them. He promises, 'Ask and it will be given you;
seek and you will find; knock and the door will be opened to
you' (Matthew 7:7).

God shows his almighty power and makes it known. Look how many times he says, 'I will' (three times in verse 6, twice in verse 8, twice in verse 10 and once in verse 12). Many of his people feel as though they are in 'a distant land' (10:9), yet he will bring them back when they remember him and call upon his name.

20.
The Good Shepherd and the foolish one

Please read Zechariah 11:1-17

Chapters 9 and 10 have told of the great victory which God is going to bring to his people, and of his watchful care over them. Now we turn to a darker side. Trouble is bound to come when people neglect God. It is so foolish to forget God and act as though we can manage on our own and are the masters of our own fate.

The prophet Zechariah is used by God to remind the Jews that they should not be complacent. They should be watchful of their lives and their possessions. There is an enemy who is waiting to invade their land. They desperately need a good and wise leader, and they should make sure that they follow his sensible leadership.

Judgement to come (11:1-3)

The direction from which this judgement will come is the north. These three verses name three areas: Lebanon, Bashan and Jordan. Lebanon is in the extreme north-west of the land, Bashan is in the north-east and the River Jordan runs through the centre of the land.

Lebanon is often in the news. There is continual ferment in that land. Muslim and 'Christian' factors are constantly warring today. As I write, various Westerners are being held hostage and Beirut has ceased to be the lovely city that it once was. Lebanon is naturally a beautiful land. Isaiah calls it a glorious place (Isaiah 35:2) and it is noted for the strength and durability of its cedar trees. 'The word Lebanon comes from the Hebrew word Leban, meaning white and the rabbis almost always referred to the temple as the House of Lebanon, because it was constructed of cedars and the beautiful white dome stood on mount Moriah.' [1]

Bashan was on the east of the Jordan and it lay to the north of Gilead. Today it is often in the news and is known as the Golan Heights. Those who occupy this area have a commanding view of all of Galilee to the south-west and Damascus to the north-east. Bashan was famous for its oak trees (Ezekiel 27:6) although there are few left now. Its forests grew thick and strong.

The Jordan is the river which links the north and the south of the land. It winds in and out for most of its distance between the Lake of Galilee in the north and the Dead Sea in the south. In places its banks were very fertile. Thick bushes and trees grew there and the tropical vegetation provided shelter for lions, among other animals. There are no lions there now but it is said that they continued to survive in these favourable conditions until some two hundred years ago.

The dense cedar trees of Lebanon, the strong oaks of Bashan and the rich foliage of the Jordan combined to protect Jerusalem and all Judea. An enemy coming from the north could easily be defeated because of the natural barrier formed by these wooded areas.

The strong barriers will be removed

The Lord Almighty spoke to Zechariah and bade him prophesy: **'Open your doors, O Lebanon'** (11:1). These strong barriers will be removed by the judgements of God. How could such strong cedars and oaks be removed? Even those who do not live in parts of the world where hurricanes and typhoons occur regularly will be aware, from the media, of the tremendous devastation caused by these forces of nature.

And when God says he is going to bring his punishment upon a land it is a foolish person who doubts his ability to do such a thing. God said to his people in Zechariah's time, 'Don't try to escape my punishment. You will not be able to do anything about it. You might just as well open your doors and let the judgement in.' Fire will destroy the great cedars (11:1). The pine trees will fall and be ruined (11:2). Rich pasture land will be destroyed (11:3). The lush habitat of the lions will be ruined (11:3), and all of this will bring great anguish upon the people.

The rulers of Israel are described as shepherds and lions (11:3). **'Listen to the wail of the shepherds.'** Why are they crying out? Because their **'rich pastures are destroyed'** (11:3). In other words, they were not so worried about the fate of the land and its people as about their loss of income. The awful thing was that the rulers of the people were not only failing to lead the people aright (as we saw in 10:2-3), they were milking them dry! They were just like the shepherds in Ezekiel 34:1-10 – only after what they could get for themselves.

The entry of the Romans

The great storm spoken of in these opening three verses represented an invasion that was going to come upon God's people. Many commentators say that this refers to the Roman invasion, which happened between the uprising of the Maccabees and the coming of the Messiah 500 years after Zechariah's time.

How did the Romans enter the land? They came in by way of Lebanon. T.V. Moore says, 'The reference is to that desolating storm of civil war that caused the calling in of the Romans, whose legions swept like a whirlwind of steel over the land, and finally prostrated every vestige of independent authority, from the cedars of Lebanon to the lowliest cypress, that refused to be subdued, and humbled the whole land beneath the mighty power of Rome.'[2]

Zechariah represents the Good Shepherd (11:4-14)

The prophet assumes the guise of the Messiah and tells this allegory (11:7-14) to warn the people of the danger they are in. God is offering them one last chance to turn back to him and his ways. The current leaders were only after gain and Judah was **'the flock marked for slaughter'** (11:4). In other words, God's flock had been singled out and were being fattened up for the market-place.

But these were not sheep, they were people! Their leaders were not looking after them. They were selling them into slavery. They were getting rich on the proceeds, and they were getting away with it! The rulers of the people were even thanking God for their rich profit. **'Those who sell them say, "Praise the Lord, I am rich"'** (11:5). Laetsch tersely comments, 'In base hypocrisy they even thank God for granting them riches and honours, while they unmercifully fleece the sheep.'[3]

At this point God sent Zechariah, representing the Messiah, to pasture, that is, to feed, the sheep (11:4). He is to be the Good Shepherd. Meanwhile, God himself rejects the people, and especially their leaders. He says that he will no longer have pity upon them because of their sinful ways. He says he will hand them over to their neighbours and their king (11:6). Many believe that this refers to the Romans. Years later the chief priests were to reject Jesus as their king and shout, 'We have no king but Caesar' (John 19:15). Therefore, God says, 'I will hand you over to the king.' Think of some of the dreadful cruelties wrought by so many of the Roman Emperors. God says, **'They will oppress the land, and I will not rescue them from their hands'** (11:6). 'Since they [the Jewish leaders] showed no pity on God's people, God will not pity them.'[4]

The Good Shepherd

As the Good Shepherd, Zechariah went about his work. **'I pastured the flock marked for slaughter, particularly the oppressed of the flock'** (11:7). He was concerned about the ordinary people of God, especially the poor and afflicted, just as the Messiah will be. Isaiah says,

> 'He tends his flock like a shepherd:
>   He gathers the lambs in his arms
> and carries them close to his heart;
>   he gently leads those that have young'
>
> (Isaiah 40:11).

We have already seen in chapter 10 that the Messiah is the Shepherd-King and we know that Jesus is called the Good Shepherd (John 10:11-18). This makes what Zechariah now proceeded to do even more remarkable.

He took two staffs. These were a shepherd's main equipment. He had a heavy stick to drive off wild animals and a crook to lean upon and to lift up fallen animals out of crevices and holes where they might have fallen. The psalmist refers to these when he says, 'Your rod and your staff, they comfort me' (Psalm 23:4). One of these staffs he names 'Favour' and the other one 'Union' (11:7).

Part of his work was to get rid of three shepherds, which he said he did in one month (11:8). Joyce Baldwin tells us that these shepherds have been identified in at least forty different ways.[5] So what hope have we of identifying them correctly? However, it seems that they refer to three kinds of leaders of the people. These were kings (rulers), priests and prophets. A month is a comparatively short time. What did Jesus do? In a short while, by his death and resurrection, he abolished all other Jewish kings, priests and prophets and replaced them by himself. He is now Prophet, Priest and King for all of his people.

The Good Shepherd rejected

The passage now takes on a very sad tone. The people rejected the Good Shepherd. The Messiah said, **'The flock detested me'** (11:8). The same kind of language is used of Isaiah's suffering servant: 'He was despised and rejected by men' (Isaiah 53:3).

It is incredible that a people who desperately needed good, strong, wise and compassionate leadership should reject the Messiah, God's chosen one. 500 years later they were to cry out, 'Crucify him, crucify him,' and to cheer when Jesus was put to death. People today still refuse the Lord Jesus Christ access to their lives, and even professing churches keep him outside of their doors because he does not measure up to their idea of the Shepherd-King.

The Good Shepherd unleashes judgement upon his people

In time the Good Shepherd **'grew weary of them'**, that is, of his people. He said, **'I will not be your shepherd. Let the dying**

die, and the perishing perish' (11:8). In other words, he is bringing to an end his providential care of the sheep. They have rejected him, so now **'Let those who are left eat one another's flesh'** (11:9). Josephus says that this actually happened during the Roman siege of Jerusalem in A.D. 70 (see also Lamentations 4:10).

Next, the Good Shepherd broke his staff called Favour (11:10). This was his agreement with all the nations to hold them back from punishing his people. The 'nations' here seem to refer particularly to the Romans, because it was certainly they who overran Israel and eventually drove the Jews from their land. This judgement came about because the Jews rejected the Messiah and 'on that day' God would revoke his agreement to protect his people (11:11).

When the disasters of A.D. 70 (the destruction of Jerusalem and the temple by the Romans) happened many were puzzled and shocked. However, there were some who had spiritual insight and recognized that it was the Lord who was punishing the people. They are described as 'the afflicted of the flock', and are the same remnant as in verse 7.

It is still the same today. Many of the religious people and the important people of the land will be shocked and surprised when they stand before the judgement seat of Christ. They will realize then that God has not called to himself many who are wise by human standards, or influential or of noble birth, 'but God chose the foolish things of the world to shame the wise; God chose the weak things of the world to shame the strong. He chose the lowly things of this world and the despised things' (1 Corinthians 1:27-28).

The last straw!

Then came the final insult to the Good Shepherd. The Messiah said, **'If you think it best, give me my pay; but if not, keep it'** (11:12). He was talking about severance pay. The relationship between the Good Shepherd and the flock of Israel was ending. 'If you don't pay me, then keep it' is an even more emphatic way of putting an end to a relationship.

'So they paid me thirty pieces of silver.' That was the price of a slave who had been gored by a bull – a dead slave (Exodus

21:32). It was a trifling amount. Notice the irony and sarcasm in the phrase, **'the handsome price at which they priced me!'** (11:13).

Then the Lord said to the Good Shepherd, **'Throw it to the potter'** (11:13). **'So I took the thirty pieces of silver and threw them into the house of the Lord to the potter.'** The potters were the poorest of the people; they were paid the least. 'They made pots that broke, and they were not skilled men like the silversmiths.'[6]

What does 'throw it to the potter' signify? Some say it is a proverbial phrase like, 'Throw it to the dogs.' Others remind us that the potter for the temple had his shop nearby in the Valley of Hinnom, because the best clay for his work was to be found there.

The Valley of Hinnom was a polluted place for Jews. It was once used for idolatry (2 Kings 23:10) and it was said that the corpses of criminals, animals and refuse of all kinds were burnt there. The name came to be used as a synonym for 'hell'. It is called 'Gehenna' in the Gospels. Therefore it was a suitable place to throw an insulting amount of money.

Jeremiah had spoken a great deal about potters. In chapter 18 he had visited a potter's house and God had told him that Israel was like clay in the hands of the potter: 'O house of Israel, can I not do with you as this potter does?' (Jeremiah 18:6). In chapter 19 he was sent to buy a clay jar from a potter and God spoke to him about coming judgement upon Israel. Where was the potter? In the 'valley of Ben Hinnom' (Jeremiah 19:6). And in chapter 32 Jeremiah was instructed to buy a field at Anathoth just as Nebuchadnezzar was about to invade the land as a token that one day God's people would again inhabit the land.

The payment to the Messiah of thirty pieces of silver and his throwing it down *in the house of the Lord* to the potter, together with Jeremiah's prophecy, reminds us of the sad events towards the end of Jesus' life on earth, when Judas Iscariot betrayed him. What was the payment that Judas received? Thirty pieces of silver (Matthew 26:15). What did Judas do when he realized how much he had sinned? He tried to return the money to the chief priests, but they refused to have it back. So what did Judas do with the money? He threw it down *in the temple* and went and hanged himself (Matthew

27:5). What did the chief priests do with the money? They could not put it in the temple treasury because it was blood money, so they decided to use the money to buy a field to bury strangers in. What was that field? It was 'the potter's field', the Field of Blood (Matthew 27:7-8). Everything concerning the Messiah was fulfilled to the letter!

Matthew said that this was the prophecy of Jeremiah which had been fulfilled (Matthew 27:9). Bible critics pounce on this and say that it is a mistake to say these were words of Jeremiah when, in fact, Zechariah prophesied this. It may be that Matthew attributed these words to Jeremiah because the prophets were all bound together in one scroll, and Jeremiah, as one of the major prophets, was the first book on the scroll. However, it may be that Matthew was referring to the field that Jeremiah purchased in chapter 32 of his prophecy.

The breaking of the second staff

Next the Good Shepherd broke the staff called 'Union'. This symbolized the ending of the unity between the north and the south of the land. It would also pave the way for the Romans to break up the Jewish nation. The Pharisees were very concerned lest the Romans should come and take away their land and nation. They told the Sanhedrin (the Jewish Council) that if they did not stop Jesus performing miraculous signs everyone would believe on him, and that would mean the end of their nation (John 11:48). This is exactly what did happen. The nation was scattered and the land was taken away from them, all because the Jews rejected the Messiah and refused to let him reign over them.

But Zechariah's acting was not finished. He had another task to perform.

Zechariah acts as a foolish shepherd (11:15-17)

God was going to raise up a foolish shepherd over the land. He is also called **'the worthless shepherd'** (11:17). This foolish shepherd is not like the Good Shepherd. He does not have the interest of the sheep at heart. He is only in it for the money.

When danger comes he runs away because 'he is a hired hand
and cares nothing for the sheep' (John 10:13).

Verse 16 tells us that this shepherd will not care for the lost.
He will not seek the young or heal the injured. He will not
even bother to feed the healthy (who need little looking
after). He is only after what he can get for himself. He will eat
the meat of the best sheep (whom he is supposed to be looking
after) and even conduct a greedy search for the last edible
morsel. He **'will eat the meat of the choice sheep, tearing off
their hoofs'** (11:16).

But this worthless shepherd will be punished, eventually.
God says, **'Woe to the worthless shepherd, who deserts the
flock! May the sword strike his arm and his right eye! May his
arm be completely withered, his right eye totally blinded!'**
(11:17). How can a shepherd do his job if his arm is completely withered and he is blind in his right eye? God is saying
that this foolish shepherd's power will be paralysed and his
intelligence become non-existent. In other words this leader
will be powerless to fight.

The Lord is our Good Shepherd

God still cares for his people and is still their Shepherd. They
need to 'know that the Lord is God. It is he who made us, and
we are his; we are his people, the sheep of his pasture' (Psalm
100:3).

How foolish it is to forget that the Lord Jesus Christ is our
Good Shepherd, our Great Shepherd and our Chief
Shepherd! We need to rejoice in his leadership of us, and our
churches need to acknowledge his authority over them.

The Evil One is active and is ever seeking to gain control
over God's people. He lures many astray, and even whole
congregations are drawn aside from the wholesome food of
God's Word. Leaders are raised up who claim to be under-
shepherds of the flock of God, yet they are seeking all the
glory for themselves. How sad it is when people refer to their
churches as 'Mr ...'s church' instead of the Lord's church!
How dangerous it is when people hang upon every word of
their pastors, without first checking that it is all in accordance
with the whole counsel of God!

In 2 Thessalonians we read of the coming of the man of lawlessness, who will 'oppose and will exalt himself over everything that is called God or is worshipped, so that he sets himself up in God's temple, proclaiming himself to be God' (2 Thessalonians 2:4). Many will follow that lawless one and even now there are many who are led astray by his predecessors. We need to examine where we and our church fellowships stand in regard to the truth. We need to stand firm in the Lord and remember that one day all evil will be cast down and we shall reign with Christ eternally.

21.
God's gifts of victory and repentance

Please read Zechariah 12:1-14

God's people often find life hard. Just as things seem to be going well, then the enemy attacks. Satan is always on the look-out to see if he can destroy, or at least afflict, those who follow the Lord.

In Zechariah 12 we see the city of Jerusalem besieged by **'all the nations of the earth** [who] **are gathered against her'**. We do not know whether the prophet is referring to any specific future event or not, but the message of these verses is that the holy city will never be utterly defeated even though many enemies gather against her to destroy her.

As in chapters 2 and 8, Jerusalem is a picture of the people of God, the church of Jesus Christ. However powerful and numerous the attackers of the church are, Jesus says, 'The gates of Hades will not overcome it' (Matthew 16:18).

God promises victory for his people (12:1-9)

The Lord reminds Israel of his great power and authority. He says that he **'stretches out the heavens'**. God made the heavens and maintains them. He controls the weather and orders it according to his purposes.

He also 'lays the foundation of the earth'. God is active. In saying this the Lord does not mean that he merely set up his creation and then gave it a push, as a child used to wind up a clockwork toy and then watch it shoot across the ground on its own. God actually created all things, controls all things and carefully watches over them.

God also 'formed the spirit of man within him'. He did not just create the wonders of nature. He created man, the highest of all creation, and sent him out into this world with the purpose of honouring the Lord and doing his will. God is the Creator and sustainer of this universe. He is in charge. Satan and all his hosts think that they are in control, but they are mistaken.

Jerusalem – a besieged city

Verses 2-6 paint the picture of Jerusalem surrounded by her many enemies, and they show what is going to happen to those who oppose God's people. The nations intend to defeat Jerusalem while she is down. After all, the inhabitants of Judah had not been back long from captivity. The city was still half built, even the temple was unfinished. And the walls were unlikely to be able to keep out any determined attacker.

But Jerusalem has a secret weapon. The Lord has his 'watchful eye' on the house of Judah (12:4). 'Whoever touches you touches the apple of his eye' (2:8). **'The people of Jerusalem are strong, because the Lord Almighty is their God'** (12:5). God, who created and orders all things, is on the side of his people. They need not fear what their enemies will do to them. Like God's people many years later, they will learn to say, 'If God is for us, who can be against us?' (Romans 8:31).

The fate of the attackers

Zechariah speaks of the attack upon Jerusalem and says what will happen **'on that day'**. 'On that day' is a phrase that occurs over and over again, and especially in the closing chapters of Zechariah's prophecy. It means, 'the day of the Lord'. It is 'a time of judgement or blessing when God intervenes decisively in the affairs of the nations'.[1]

Firstly, the attackers will be rendered impotent. They will approach Jerusalem thinking that they have an easy task before them. It will take little effort to conquer this weak city!

But God says, **'I am going to make Jerusalem a cup that sends all the surrounding peoples reeling'** (12:2). In other words, when the enemies attack Jerusalem they will become like drunken men. They will be unable to do what they set out to do. They will stagger from side to side and will not be able to think clearly.

Secondly, the attackers will injure themselves. **'On that day, when all the nations of the earth are gathered against her, I will make Jerusalem an immovable rock for all the nations. All who try to move it will injure themselves'** (12:3). The enemies of Jerusalem will want to get rid of the city. It is like a large stone which a farmer finds embedded in the soil, and hinders him in the ploughing of his field. But when the farmer tries to lift it, he finds that it is far too heavy for him and he 'puts his back out' or the stone tumbles sideways and falls heavily on to his toe and damages it. In the same way, the nations of the earth who are gathered against Jerusalem will find her immovable and, in trying to defeat her, will themselves be injured.

Thirdly, the horses of the cavalry will panic. **'On that day I will strike every horse with panic and its rider with madness'** (12:4). The horse was the main weapon of attack. God will cause confusion to the attackers and they will not be able to achieve their goal. The Lord says, **'I will blind all the horses of the nations.'** As a result the nations will end up fighting each other. Haggai had earlier prophesied that the Lord would 'overthrow chariots and their drivers; horses and their riders will fall, each by the sword of his brother' (Haggai 2:22).

Fourthly, the leaders of Judah will destroy their attackers. They will set fire to them. They will be like a flaming 'brazier in a woodpile, like a flaming torch among sheaves. They will consume right and left all the surrounding peoples, but Jerusalem will remain intact in her place' (12:6).

What is the meaning of this for today?

The church of Jesus Christ is like a strong city, 'the holy place where the Most High dwells. God is within her, she will not fall' (Psalm 46:4-5). Satan and his hosts regard the church as a cup which can easily be drained and then thrown away. This cup, however, shall prove to be a cup of trembling to them. 'They shall tremble with disappointment and helpless rage at their failure to destroy the church, with fear and terror as they behold the judgements of God coming upon the enemies of the church.'[2]

There is a day coming when Satan will make one last all-out effort against God's people. We should be prepared for his onslaught. However, we should not tremble, as we did in the last war when Hitler was poised at Calais waiting to pounce upon Britain to defeat her. We should remember that the Lord is with us. Christ has already gained the victory over Satan when he triumphed on the cross of Calvary.

But God's people will not only be able to defend themselves, they will be able to take the initiative too. The leaders of God's church will go out with his people into the world with the gospel message and it will spread like wildfire.

The dwellings of Judah

The people living in the land surrounding the city of Jerusalem did not have the protection or the prestige of the capital city. Usually the open country and small towns of Judah were the first to be taken by the enemy. The inhabitants of Judah lived a lowly existence and were sometimes looked down upon by the citizens of Jerusalem. It is these humble people who will have the privilege of being delivered first when the enemy attacks. **'The Lord will save the dwellings [tents] of Judah first, so that the honour of the house of David and of Jerusalem's inhabitants may not be greater than that of Judah'** (12:7).

Jerusalem has the honour of being a symbol of the city of God, but there should be no room for pride here. Think of the life of Jesus. The Messiah was not born in Jerusalem, but in Bethlehem. The centre of his ministry was Capernaum and Galilee, not Jerusalem; he only paid occasional visits to the capital. 'In the Christian church there is to be no superiority of city over country, of capital city over others, of large congregations over gatherings of two or three. Not locality or size, but Christ and his word represent the true glory of congregations and churches.'[3]

The protection of Jerusalem

The words in verse 5, **'The people of Jerusalem are strong, because the Lord Almighty is their God',** are seen to be true in verses 8 and 9. **'On that day the Lord will shield those who live in Jerusalem, so that the feeblest among them will be like David, and the house of David will be like God, like the Angel of the Lord going before them. On that day I will set out to destroy all nations that attack Jerusalem.'**

God's people are one, whether they dwell in the open countryside with no more protection for them than fragile tents, or whether they live in strong houses. God's people are one, whether they are rulers or peasants. God has his protective shield over them. Even the weakest of the people will be brave like David, the giant-killer. And from the house of David shall come one who is called 'the Lord our righteousness' (Jeremiah 23:5-6). God, the Angel of the Lord, will go before God's people and destroy every enemy who dares to rise against the church of the redeemed.

God promises repentance for his people (12:10-14)

God not only gives victory to his people but he gives a spirit of penitence. The victory of Jerusalem and Judah will lead to humility, not pride.

Verse 10 says, **'And** [in addition to the victory] **I will pour out on the house of David and the inhabitants of Jerusalem a spirit of grace and supplication.'** 'Pouring out' speaks of an abundant flow. When God promises to pour out blessings he is not niggardly or stingy with his gifts. He is generous and bounteous in bestowing his grace upon his people. This is surely a foreshadowing of the pouring out of God's Spirit at Pentecost (in Acts 2).

Grace and supplication are God's free gifts. They cannot be earned or merited in any way. Indeed, it is 'because of the Lord's great love we are not consumed' (Lamentations 3:22). We deserve to be destroyed because within ourselves there is nothing good, only that which God has placed within us. '"Grace" indicates the motive that prompts the out-pouring of the divine Spirit. "Supplication" indicates the result that will follow it.'[4]

Who will receive these blessings?

God says that those who receive these blessings are they who **'will look on me'** (12:10). What will they see when they look upon the Lord? They will see one who has been pierced. Believers will look in faith to God and discover that he has been grievously wounded. But worse follows. **'They will look on me, the one they have pierced.'** They will realize, with horror, that their own sin and impurity (13:1) have caused the Lord to be hurt.

This can refer to none other than the Messiah. It was God's own Son, the Lord Jesus Christ, who was wounded, pierced and hung up to die upon the cruel cross of Calvary. John 19:33-37 describes how one of the soldiers pierced Jesus' side with a spear to make sure that he was dead; and John quotes Zechariah 12:10 to show that the prophecy is being partly fulfilled by this act.

For believers in the Lord Jesus Christ this verse in Zechariah makes uncomfortable reading. The awful thing is that there was a time when we rejected the Lord, just as the flock deserted the Good Shepherd in Zechariah 11:8. Our rejection of Christ wounded him. Because God's people sinned, Jesus had to die. When the house of David and the inhabitants of Jerusalem look upon the one they have pierced they will realize the enormity of their sin and the grievous damage they have done to the Holy One of God.

A time of great mourning

'They will mourn for him as one mourns for an only child, and grieve bitterly for him as one grieves for a first-born son' (12:10).

Think of the most dreadful calamity that could befall you. Consider the grief that would overcome you were that to happen. Those of us who have lost a child know what it is to grieve and mourn like this. It is not something which any parent gets over quickly. To lose an *only* child must be a very bitter pill to swallow! But 'God so loved the world that *he gave* his one and only Son, that whoever believes in him shall not perish but have eternal life' (John 3:16).

This is how God's people will behave when they realize the enormity of their sin. **'The weeping...will be great, like the weeping of Hadad Rimmon in the plain of Megiddo'** (12:11). Josiah was the last godly king of Judah. He was much loved by his people and in the year 609 B.C. he went out to fight a battle against Pharaoh Neco. In the battle he was fatally wounded. He died when he was taken back to Jerusalem (2 Chronicles 35:20-24) and his death caused great lamentation throughout the whole land. The people wept greatly because he was their king. But they also wept for themselves because they realized that with his death their fate was practically sealed, their days were numbered. Nebuchadnezzar was soon on their doorstep!

A private mourning

'The land will mourn, each clan by itself, with their wives by themselves: the clan of the house of David and their wives, the clan of the house of Nathan and their wives, the clan of the house of Levi and their wives, the clan of Shimei and their wives, and all the rest of the clans and their wives' (12:12-14).

This weeping is not a display in order to attract attention to the supposed holiness of the mourners. They will not be like the hypocrites who liked to 'pray standing in the synagogues and on the street corners to be seen by men' (Matthew 6:5). These Jews will be so ashamed of their sin that they will creep away on their own, 'each clan by itself'. Even the wives will mourn separately from their husbands.

As the prophet looks he sees **'the land'**, the holy land, the church, 'every family apart' (12:12 AV) weeping for the one who has been pierced. 'No family and no individual will be satisfied to have others mourn in their stead. There is no vicarious mourning or substitutionary repentance in God's church.'[5] The clan of the house of David mourned and the clan of his less well-known son Nathan grieved also. The clans of the priests mourned, the clan of well-known Levi and the clan of his almost unknown grandson Shimei all wept. And **'all the rest of the clans and their wives'** mourned. No one was left out.

In their prayers and supplications before the throne of God all believers are equal; none received special privilege or priority because of rank or influence or sex. Each one, who-ever they are, has to come and confess his or her sin and base-ness. Their sins have pierced and slain the Lord. As they look on the Lord and see him wounded for their transgressions, they weep. The closer any believer gets to the Lord, the more he feels his own unworthiness. When Peter became aware of the power and majesty of Jesus, 'he fell at Jesus' knees and said, "Go away from me, Lord; I am a sinful man!"' (Luke 5:8). There is no room for pride or selfishness when faced with the crucified Christ. Jerusalem might be an important city. Judah's leaders may be highly favoured. God has done great things for them, but none has any cause for self-con-gratulation because it is the Lord who has gained the victory.

The need for individual repentance

The city of God, the church of the redeemed, will gain the vic-tory by the substitutionary death of the Lord Jesus Christ; but as with Jerusalem, the church is made up of men, women and children. No one can be a member of God's church without first coming as an individual and confessing his or her sin, without being brought to a true repentance and having faith in the Lord Jesus Christ for salvation.

C.H. Spurgeon preached a sermon on 16 July 1885 on Zechariah 12:12-14. He spoke of the need for individual repentance for sin. He said, 'Sham repentance can do its work in the mass; it talks about national sin and national sorrow, which generally means the mere notion of sin and the notion of repentance. But when it comes to a true work of the Spirit of God, and men really do mourn for sin so as to obtain par-don, it is a thing in which each individual stands in a personal solitude, as much apart from everybody else as if he had been the sole man that God ever made...and had himself so sinned that the whole anger of God for sin had fallen upon him.'[6]

There must be conviction of, and godly sorrow for sin before anyone can truly become an inhabitant of God's holy city – the church of Jesus Christ.

22.
Pardon and its consequences

Please read Zechariah 13:1-9

In chapter 12 of Zechariah's prophecy we saw how Jerusalem was being besieged by invaders from the nations. The city proved to be like an immovable rock to their enemies (12:3). Verses 10 to 14 record what happened when the Lord poured out on the house of David and the inhabitants of Jerusalem a spirit of grace and supplication: there was great mourning.

In Zechariah 13:1 we are shown the reason for all the weeping: it was because of the **'sin and impurity'** of the Jewish people. In this chapter we see God's provision of pardon for sin, and are given instructions on how forgiven people should behave as a result of their cleansing from sin.

Cleansing from sin (13:1)

This is what sensible people desire. They come to realize that one day they will be judged. Things are not right in their nation. There are deficiencies which need to be made up. Worse than that there is the whole problem of sin which is keeping them from communion with God.

For God's people, one of the first steps out of this dreadful situation is to become aware that their sin has sent the Lord Jesus Christ to the cruel cross of Calvary. If they had not sinned, then Jesus would not have had to die. They become so convinced of this that they will look upon Jesus, the one they have pierced (12:10), and they will weep bitterly because of their sin. Sin is not a light thing and it cannot be overlooked. It must be dealt with.

A fountain will be opened

'On that day a fountain will be opened to the house of David
and the inhabitants of Jerusalem, to cleanse them from sin
and impurity' (13:1). In chapter 12:11 we read, 'On that
day...weeping'. Here we read, **'On that day...a fountain'.**
This word 'fountain' means something which is always flowing. It is provided not to quench thirst but to cleanse from sin.
It is something which is 'opened'. It has been 'dug out', and it
provides a constant, abundant supply of cleansing power.

This special fountain will be for the cleansing of 'sin and
impurity'. It is that which meets the urgent need of penitent
(weeping) sinners. Sin is that which 'misses the mark'; it 'falls
short of the glory of God' (Romans 3:23). And impurity is a
word which sums up all those things which are dishonouring
to God, those things which defile mankind.

In Old Testament times there was already a system for cov-
ering over sin and uncleanness. Sacrifices were offered (as
detailed in Leviticus chapters 1 to 7). However, the problem
was that sacrifices had to be offered continually. They only
provided a temporary solution to the problem of sin. It was
not until God provided the perfect Lamb of God that the
problem of sin could be dealt with once and for all.

Cleansing by this fountain is open to the house of David and
the inhabitants of Jerusalem. It is not just for the leaders of
the people of God. It is opened for all of the inhabitants of the
city, however insignificant and poor they might be. It is
opened for all who look to the Lord Jesus Christ for cleansing
from their sin. It is opened to all who believe in the Lord Jesus
Christ.

William Cowper summed it up like this:

> There is a fountain filled with blood
>   Drawn from Immanuel's veins;
> And sinners plunged beneath that flood
>   Lose all their guilty stains.

The sad fact is that those who reject Christ (the Good
Shepherd of chapter 11) are refusing to be cleansed from their
sin.

The consequences of cleansing (13:2-6)

Changes have to be made when people are cleansed from their sin and impurity. God declares, 'Once you have been justified (made righteous), you need to be sanctified (the process of being made holy).' This is a lifelong procedure. God's people are required to live holy lives and they should strive after a life given over entirely to God and obedience to his commands. The message here is the same as that which has been spoken over and over again to the Jews. God's people are required to turn their backs upon their old lives and to start anew.

There were two major evils in the land – idolatry and false prophets.

Idolatry

'"**On that day, I will banish the names of the idols from the land, and they will be remembered no more," declares the Lord Almighty**' (13:2). Idolatry was the constant problem of Israel. They kept turning their backs on their God and turning towards false idols. They wanted to worship something they could see. Now God says that even the names of these idols will be banished from among them.

Idols had been given the people's devotion. But those who have been cleansed from their sin should now be in love with God. Anything which takes from us the affection which belongs to God alone should be banished from our lives.

Anyone whom the people of God love will be given their time. Anyone whom a believer loves will be given his affection. Anyone whom a church loves will be given its money. And anyone whom a Christian loves will occupy a large place in his or her thoughts. Today the Lord's people need to be asked, 'Is there anyone who claims more of your time, love, gifts and thoughts than the Lord Jesus Christ?' Anything which comes between God's people and the Lord is an idol and it needs to be torn down from its throne so that the Lord alone can be worshipped.

False prophets

God says, 'Now that you have been cleansed from your sin you must stop receiving guidance from those who are not my servants.' **'I will remove both the prophets and the spirit of impurity from the land. And if anyone still prophesies, his father and mother, to whom he was born, will say to him, "You must die, because you told lies in the Lord's name." When he prophesies, his own parents will stab him'** (13:2-3).

'Idolatry was the prime cause of the land's defilement. But without the false prophet such substitute-gods could not have flourished.'[1]

In Deuteronomy 13:6-11 we read that close relatives had to be the first to stone to death anyone who enticed God's people to worship false gods. In the days of Jesus there were many false prophets who tried to lead the people astray. Today we need to be on our guard against those who claim to have special revelations from God. Those who teach things which are contrary to God's Word are false and they must be turned out of the church until they repent and desire to return in humility. (We no longer stone false prophets!)

In the days to come, those who have not truly been called by God will be ashamed to be recognized as prophets. **'On that day every prophet will be ashamed of his prophetic vision. He will not put on a prophet's garment of hair in order to deceive. He will say, "I am not a prophet. I am a farmer; the land has been my livelihood since my youth"'** (13:4-5).

Sometimes prophets wore special clothing. In the case of Elijah, Elisha and John the Baptist we know that the 'badge' of a prophet was a hairy garment. But 'on that day' false prophets will pretend that they are farm workers, and always have been. Perhaps they will try to give the impression that they were sold into slavery as children because of their father's debts. They will deny all marks of a prophet.

'What about those wounds in your body? Aren't they those with which prophets afflict themselves when they are in an ecstatic trance?' one of God's people might ask. 'No', the false prophet will reply, 'I got them in a drunken brawl,' or he might say, 'These are the marks of discipline which I received from my parents when they sought to correct my bad behaviour.'

'In that day' the false prophet will be more ashamed to admit that he was a prophet than he will be to say that he was a drunkard. **'If someone asks him, "What are these wounds on your body?" he will answer, "The wounds I was given at the house of my friends"'** (13:6).

The death of the Good Shepherd (13:7-9)

There now follows a poem about the one whom God calls 'my shepherd'. Remember that a shepherd is a leader and provider for his people; Old Testament kings were often called shepherds.

In chapter 11:8 we read that the Good Shepherd was rejected and badly treated. Now we see even worse happening to him. The sword of judgement is used against the Good Shepherd. **'"Awake, O sword, against my shepherd, against the man who is close to me!" declares the Lord Almighty. "Strike the shepherd, and the sheep will be scattered, and I will turn my hands against the little ones"'** (13:7).

The shepherd is struck and his sheep are scattered. Who is this shepherd? He is described as 'the man who is close to me'. The Lord Almighty says this. Who is close to God? The Messiah, the Lord Jesus Christ. He is God's Son, God himself.

We need not be puzzled at the meaning of this poem because Jesus himself explains the prophecy for us. He quoted part of this seventh verse just before he was arrested and his disciples ran away. 'Jesus told them, "This very night you will all fall away on account of me, for it is written: 'I will strike the shepherd, and the sheep of the flock will be scattered'"' (Matthew 26:31). God says, 'I will strike the shepherd.' It was all part of God's plan that wicked hands should put Jesus to death by nailing him to a cross (Acts 2:23). In John 10, where he speaks of the Good Shepherd and his sheep, Jesus repeatedly says, 'I will lay down my life for the sheep.' It was part of God's scheme of salvation that his innocent Son should be put to death for his people's sins.

As a result of the shepherd being struck, the sheep were scattered. All the disciples fled when Jesus was arrested. They thought they had no leader when Jesus was put to death. But God 'turned his hands against the little ones'. This literally means, 'God will come to the aid of his "little ones" – the ones who are faithful to him.' He will encourage and help them in their trials and testing times.

A remnant will be left

With all the destruction going on there will still be a remnant left. **'Two-thirds will be struck down and perish; yet one third will be left in'** the whole land (13:8). This literally happened when the Romans wrought havoc in the land in A.D. 70. 'When Titus destroyed Jerusalem 1,500,000 Jews died by sword, pestilence and famine.'[2] But one third will be saved.

However, even those who are spared will be tried. **'This third I will bring into the fire; I will refine them like silver and test them like gold'** (13:9). God is saying, 'As precious metals are boiled to remove the dross, so my people will have their faith tested in the fires of affliction until they are pure.' Malachi had a similar message when he asked, 'But who can endure the day of his coming? Who can stand when he appears? For he will be like a refiner's fire or a launderer's soap. He will sit as a refiner and purifier of silver; he will purify the Levites and refine them like gold and silver' (Malachi 3:2-3).

God's people are often perplexed because trouble comes upon them. They say, 'What have I done to displease the Lord? Where have I gone wrong?' But so often God does not send trouble upon his people to punish them; he sends it to purify them, to sanctify them, to make them holy. He takes away all the things upon which his people lean for support, until they learn to trust in him alone. The brook dried up for Elijah, not so that God might punish him but so that he had to lean only upon the Lord (1 Kings 17:7). God tests his people so that they can, eventually, be presented to him 'without stain or wrinkle or any other blemish, but holy and blameless' (Ephesians 5:27).

The confirmation of the covenant

This godly remnant, who have been brought through the fires of affliction, will then call on the name of the Lord (13:9). They will call upon him because they know him. They belong to him. They are in covenant relationship with him.

And when they call, he will graciously answer them and confirm his covenant with them. He will say, **'They are my people.'** Then the resounding affirmation will echo back to heaven, **'The Lord is our God.'**

We must clear out the rubbish

When God cleanses a people from sin and impurity he expects them to do all they can to press on towards holiness. They must continually look backward with thankfulness to that fountain which has been opened for them. They must regularly remember their deliverance from the awfulness of the slavery of sin, and they must look to that one who cleansed them, and who keeps on cleansing them from their sin.

God's people today have the Lord's Supper as a memorial feast for their spiritual benefit. Jesus said, 'This is my body, which is for you; do this in remembrance of me...This cup is the new covenant in my blood; do this, whenever you drink it, in remembrance of me' (1 Corinthians 11:24-25). As often as they take part in the communion service, they do it in memory of Jesus their Lord and Saviour.

God's people need continually to root out from their lives and their church fellowships those unhealthy practices which hold them back from making spiritual progress. A people which makes an idol of their pastor or their glorious past history needs to do some radical pruning. A church which neglects the Bible as the only source of revelation, and listens to other voices which claim to speak with authority, is in a sad situation.

There needs to be a good clear-out of rubbish. The purifying fire of the Holy Spirit must come into their situation and burn up everything which is false so that of those who are left the Lord will be able to say, 'They are my people.'

23.
The Lord comes and reigns

Please read Zechariah 14:1-21

This last chapter in the prophecy of Zechariah paints a broad picture of the problems and ultimate blessings of God's people. As with the beginning of chapter 12, the scene is again the city of Jerusalem which is surrounded, and being threatened, by many nations. The picture is of the church being attacked by Satan and all his evil hosts.

Those who watch sport on television seem to delight in seeing the action replays of the goals in football and the fall of wickets in cricket. These moments are shown in rapid succession, each one from a slightly different angle. The reason for this is so that as full a picture as possible may be understood by the spectator. Zechariah 14 is a kind of action replay of chapters 12 and 13, shown from a different perspective.

Jerusalem surrounded by all the nations (14:1-2)

We see the plight of the people. Zechariah says that many of their possessions will be taken from them: **'A day of the Lord is coming when your plunder will be divided among you'** (14:1). This does not mean that their possessions will be divided between them but, as the RSV puts its, 'The spoil taken from you will be divided in the midst of you.' In other words, their possessions will be taken from them and, as they watch, they will see the nations helping themselves to the goods which really belong to the inhabitants of Jerusalem.

Notice the way in which Jerusalem will be dealt with: **'The city will be captured, the houses ransacked, and the women raped'** (14:2). Not only will these dreadful calamities befall them but **'Half of the city will go into exile'** (14:2). From chapter 13:8 we have seen that two thirds of the inhabitants had already died. Now, half of the remaining third will be taken away. **'But the rest of the people will not be taken from the city'** (14:2).

This is a very distressing situation for any people. How can Jerusalem survive such an ordeal? Their numbers were fairly few to begin with because they had been in captivity for seventy years and only about 50,000 people had returned to the land initially, followed by other detachments.

The meaning of these opening verses

This description of an attack upon Jerusalem fits no account of any event recorded in history. Therefore, it seems likely that this is a symbolic account of the things which are to befall Jerusalem in the last days. Remember that Jerusalem is a picture of the church of Jesus Christ, and all the nations represent Satan and his many evil hosts who constantly attack God's people. I believe this is a description of the church in the New Testament era, the gospel age (i.e. from the days of Acts 2 right up until the end of this present age).

Think of the condition of the church today. Satan has done his worst. He has plundered the church. That means that the church has been deprived of her most treasured possessions. One way in which this has happened is in regard to the purity of the gospel. The gospel has been contaminated and watered down because some of the doctrines of God's Word are unacceptable to 'modern Christians'. The purity of the gospel has been plundered because in so many places of worship it has ceased to be preached in its fulness and its freeness. People are told that it is no longer by grace alone that they must be saved, but it is also vital to observe certain ceremonies if they are to have any hope of eternal life. Grace has to be mixed with good works before a person can be saved.

In certain periods of her history the church has been taken over by those who prevented the ordinary people from reading the Bible for themselves. Only church leaders were authorized to give the accepted meaning of the Word of God.

Some of the people of God have been raped. Satan has so

ravaged many that they are not sure to whom they belong. They have been so bruised and battered that they find it almost impossible to read the Bible with understanding, and prayer is an almost meaningless exercise.

The description of the devastation of Jerusalem in verses 1 and 2 is a picture of the depleted church of Jesus Christ in our day. But, despite the gloom, verse 2 gives us hope. There is a remnant left. Not all have been taken away or polluted. Those who are left are true to God and his Word. They obey him and follow his commands.

Why has God allowed this devastation?

God allows trouble to come upon his people because they are in great need. He knows all things and, as with the church at Ephesus, by and large the church today has 'forsaken [its] first love' (Revelation 2:4). It has grown lukewarm about the things of God (Revelation 3:15-16). There is something wrong with the people of God. They have lost their love for the Lord. They have found the things of God as unpalatable as a drink of tepid water on a humid day. And God says that he is going to punish his own loved ones. Peter says, 'It is time for judgement to begin with the family of God; and if it begins with us, what will the outcome be for those who do not obey the gospel of God?' (1 Peter 4:17).

The Lord says, **'I will gather all the nations to Jerusalem, to fight against it'** (14:2). Why does God punish his people? He does it for the same reason that any caring parent disciplines his or her wayward son or daughter. Proverbs 3:11-12 still holds good: 'My son, do not despise the Lord's discipline and do not resent his rebuke, because the Lord disciplines those he loves, as a father the son he delights in.' God punishes his people because he wants to bring them back to himself. He has never stopped loving them, and he longs for them to be back in a right relationship with himself.

God will be King over the whole earth (14:3-15)

God is going to do something great. **'The Lord will go out and fight against those nations, as he fights in the day of battle'**

(14:3). Those who first heard this message would have remembered what God had done for them in the past. He had done many mighty things for them. At the banks of the Red Sea he had cried out, 'Do not be afraid. Stand firm and you will see the deliverance the Lord will bring you today' (Exodus 14:14). As the Israelites had looked, they had seen the Red Sea dividing and allowing them to escape from their enemies on dry ground. Now, says Zechariah, God is going to cause a mountain to divide so as to leave a valley running from east to west. This will be the means whereby the people of God, in the future, can make their escape from their foes. **'On that day his feet will stand on the Mount of Olives, east of Jerusalem, and the Mount of Olives will be split in two from east to west, forming a great valley, with half of the mountain moving north and half moving south. You will flee by my mountain valley, for it will extend to Azel. You will flee as you fled from the earthquake in the days of Uzziah king of Judah** [see Amos 1:1]. **Then the Lord my God will come, and all the holy ones with him'** (14:4-5).

The Mount of Olives

This mountain faces Jerusalem at its eastern end. The valley of Kidron is in between the walls of Jerusalem and this hill, and Olivet is some 200 feet higher than the city. The Lord's feet will stand on this mountain 'on that day'. It was from this mountain that the Lord took his stand when, in Ezekiel's vision (Ezekiel 11:23), the glory of the Lord departed from the temple. It was from this same mountain that the Lord Jesus Christ was taken up into heaven (Acts 1:12). What did the angels say to the surprised disciples as Jesus ascended from their sight? 'This same Jesus, who has been taken from you into heaven, will come back in the same way as you have seen him go into heaven.' Obviously there is a strong connection between Zechariah 14:4 and Acts 1:11.

The last days

I believe that verses 3-15 refer to the events which will

culminate in the new age. **'The Lord my God will come, and all the holy ones with him'** (14:5). Zechariah is so caught up with the wonder of God's people's deliverance from their enemies and the coming of the Lord in triumph that he calls him 'my God'. The Lord is going to come with all his holy angels and the company of his redeemed saints who have 'died in the Lord'.

A unique day (14:6-7)

'On that day there will be no light, no cold or frost. It will be a unique day, without daytime or night-time – a day known to the Lord. When evening comes, there will be light' (14:6-7). Everything will change. Many of the prophets described this day in similar terms (see Joel 3:15; Isaiah 13:10; 24:23). Jesus himself said, 'The sun will be darkened and the moon will not give its light; the stars will fall from the sky, and the heavenly bodies will be shaken. At that time men will see the Son of Man coming in clouds with great power and glory' (Mark 13:24-26). There will be an unusual, ethereal light.

'When evening comes, there will be light.' When evening comes it usually gets dark. It certainly does in the natural sense. And when the evening time of life comes upon people they find that it gets darker: their eyesight fades, their minds are not so bright as they were, and there is a general onset of darker days. But, as at creation, God says, 'There will be light,' because Jesus, the light of the world, is coming again.

Living water (14:8)

'On that day living water will flow out from Jerusalem, half to the eastern sea and half to the western sea, in summer and in winter' (14:8). This is not stagnant water which is spoken of, nor water which had been kept in a musty reservoir. This will be a constant supply of bubbling water from a well or fountain. The small spring of Gihon and other water supplies in Jerusalem had difficulty in satisfying the needs of the population during the long hot summers. But when the Lord comes there will be living water, in summer as well as in winter. This water will flow to the Dead Sea (in the east) to revitalize it and also to the Mediterranean Sea (in the west); the two seas will be linked together.

The Lord will be king over the whole earth (14:9)

'On that day there will be one Lord, and his name the only name' (14:9). He will not just reign over Jerusalem, but he will be king over all. Every day the Jews quote the *Shema:* 'Hear, O Israel: the Lord our God, the Lord is one. Love the Lord your God with all your heart and with all your soul and with all your strength' (Deuteronomy 6:4-5). There is a day coming when the whole world will acknowledge the lordship of Christ and the authority of his reign. 'The earth shall be filled with the glory of God, as the waters cover the sea.'[1] Paul describes it like this: 'At the name of Jesus every knee [shall] bow, in heaven and on earth and under the earth, and every tongue confess that Jesus Christ is Lord, to the glory of God the Father' (Philippians 2:10-11). And Isaac Watts says,

> Jesus shall reign where'er the sun
> Doth his successive journeys run,
> His kingdom stretch from shore to shore
> Till moons shall wax and wane no more.

Jerusalem will be elevated above the surrounding land (14:10)

'Jerusalem is in a hollow with the various hills around it all higher than the actual city which, although on the hills, lies in a sort of basin.'[2] Zechariah prophesied that the whole geographical area will alter. The surrounding hills will become a plain like Arabah. Arabah is the broad valley which runs down the whole country on both sides of the river Jordan and continues down to Elat on the Red Sea coast. This level will extend from Geba (five or six miles north of Jerusalem, on the northern border of Judah) to Rimmon (on the southern boundary of Judah). This lowering of the hills surrounding Jerusalem will naturally leave Jerusalem as an elevated place, a focal point for the whole area. Not only that, but Jerusalem itself will be raised up. Isaiah spoke of these upheavals in chapter 40 verse 3: 'Every valley shall be raised up, every mountain and hill made low; the rough ground shall become level, the rugged places a plain.' Despite all this Jerusalem will **'remain in its place'** (14:10).

The church of Jesus Christ will be lifted out of the valley of doubt, fear, dejection and despondency and will be raised up to confident hope and assurance of God's grace and life eternal. It will be built upon its eternal foundation, the Lord Jesus Christ, the immovable rock (see 12:3). It will be inhabited; never again will it be destroyed. 'Jerusalem will be secure' (14:11). Isaiah and Micah also saw these days:

> 'In the last days
> the mountain of the Lord's temple will be established
>   as chief among the mountains;
> it will be raised above the hills,
>   and peoples will stream to it.
>   Many nations will come and say,
> "Come let us go up to the mountain of the Lord,
>   to the house of the God of Jacob.
> He will teach us his ways,
>   so that we may walk in his paths."
> The law will go out from Zion,
>   the word of the Lord from Jerusalem'
>
> (Micah 4:1-2; see also Isaiah 2:2-4).

The enemies of God will be defeated (14:12-15)

These verses sketch in gruesome detail the horrible fate which awaits those who oppose the Lord and his people: **'Their flesh will rot while they are still standing on their feet, their eyes will rot in their sockets, and their tongues will rot in their mouths'** (14:12). These people had been making a stand against the people of God. They had been using their eyes to spy upon them and they had been speaking all kinds of evil against them. The plague with which the Lord will strike these enemies of his people will be like horrendous nuclear radiation. As a result these opponents of God's people will no longer be able to stand, see or speak anything, good or evil.

A rottenness had overcome them, as will overtake all who are enemies of God in 'that day'.

'On that day men will be stricken by the Lord with great panic. Each man will seize the hand of another, and they will attack each other' (14:13). We have seen this kind of confusion spoken of several times in Zechariah and in Haggai. Plague and panic will do the work of destruction upon God's enemies. The inhabitants of Judah will go into the city and fight side by side with the people of Jerusalem (14:14). Then the wealth of the nations will be added to that which was taken from the inhabitants of Jerusalem (14:1) and it will all be given to God's people. **'The wealth of all the surrounding nations will be collected – great quantities of gold and silver and clothing'** (14:14).

Even the means of transportation will be taken away from the invaders so that they cannot escape God's judgement: **'A similar plague will strike the horses and mules, the camels and donkeys, and all the animals in those camps'** (14:15). How foolish it is for a people to oppose the Lord! They will surely be punished severely (see Revelation 6:12-17).

The final blessings of God's kingdom (14:16-21)

After the battle many Gentiles will make their way up to Jerusalem: **'The survivors from all the nations that have attacked Jerusalem will go up ...'** These once were enemies but now they have been converted to the ways of the true God. They will go regularly to Jerusalem, **'year after year'**, not to attack it but 'to worship the King, the Lord Almighty, and to celebrate the Feast of Tabernacles' (14:16).

The Feast of Tabernacles

Why is the Feast of Tabernacles singled out? It reminds the Jews of their time in the wilderness. During this eight-day festival modern-day Jews live in booths. These are leafy structures which they construct in their gardens or on the balconies of their flats. Sometimes a shed is built in such a way that its roof can be hinged back and flung open to the skies. This space is then decorated with branches, leaves and flowers. Often fruit is also hung from the false ceiling. It is obviously much more practical to live in a booth in Israel than it is in colder countries.

The Feast of Tabernacles is also the Jewish harvest festival. 'It reminds them that God brought them out of a dry desert into a glorious land flowing with milk and honey; a land of broad rivers and streams.'[3] It was during the last and greatest day of this feast that Jesus 'stood and said in a loud voice, "If anyone is thirsty, let him come to me and drink. Whoever believes in me, as the Scripture has said, streams of living water will flow from within him"' (John 7:37-38). It is also interesting to note that the professing church especially remembers the resurrection of Jesus on the eighth day of Holy Week.

Holiness (14:20-21)

In the new age everything will be holy. Even the bells on the horses will be inscribed with **'holy to the Lord'** (14:20). This was the phrase which was engraved upon the high priest's turban (Exodus 28:36-38) as a reminder of his consecration to the Lord's service.

Everything will be dedicated to the Lord in his blessed kingdom. The horses 'no longer needed for war will bear the inscription in their jingling harness as they provide transport for pilgrims'.[4]

'Every pot in Jerusalem and Judah will be holy to the Lord Almighty' (14:21). Even common things become holy when they are used for God's service. 'A cooking pot from any kitchen in the capital or the country would be good enough to boil a sacrifice in.'[5]

No Canaanites in the Lord's house (14:21)

'There will no longer be a Canaanite in the house of the Lord Almighty.' The Canaanites were the original inhabitants of the land. They served other gods. They represent anyone who is morally or spiritually unclean. There will be no room for people like that in God's kingdom – unless they become completely transformed! In speaking of heaven John says, 'Nothing impure will ever enter it, nor will anyone who does what is shameful or deceitful, but only those whose names are written in the Lamb's book of life' (Revelation 21:27).

God is still on the throne

God's kingdom is a reality. While the people of God are living in the gospel age, the going is proving to be tough. The enemy is constantly attacking everything that is set up for the Lord's glory. Yet there is a blessed day ahead when the Lord Jesus Christ will come again. A new age will be established. There will be a new heaven and a new earth. The Holy City, the new Jerusalem, will be the dwelling-place of God; and his people, the new Israel (born-again Jews *and* Gentiles), will live with him and share in the splendour of his temple. Each of God's people will be given a new name and they will sing a new song. In that heavenly city God says, 'I am making everything new!' (Revelation 21:5). And everything will be 'holy to the Lord'.

God's people should not be too despondent about the attacks of the Evil One. 'God is still on the throne.' He is in control. The devil will endeavour to persuade the people of God that the city of God will perish, but Satan is a liar. The Lord's people need to remember the promises of this prophecy of Zechariah. There might well be many mountains of difficulty standing in the way, trying to stop the progress of God's work, but he has said, '"It is not by might nor by power, but by my Spirit," says the Lord Almighty' (Zechariah 4:6). When a people fall on their knees and in humility confess their sin and seek God's forgiveness, he graciously comes upon them and by the power of his Spirit enables them to be 'more than conquerors'. God's people need to remember regularly that 'The Lord will be king over the whole earth' (Zechariah 14:9).

References

Chapter 1
1. Joyce Baldwin, *Haggai and Malachi, (Tyndale Commentary),* IVP, 1972, p. 28.
2. Robert Hawker, *The Minor Prophets,* Sherwood, Neeley and Jones, 1812, p. 477.
3. For a discussion on why the Old Testament prophets decreased in number see H. L. Ellison, *Men Spake from God,* Paternoster Press, 1966, pp. 117-8.
4. R. K. Harrison, *Introduction to the Old Testament,* IVP, 1970, p. 944.
5. D. J. Wiseman, *The New Bible Commentary,* Third Edition, IVP, 1970, p. 781.
6. T. V. Moore, *Haggai and Malachi,* Banner of Truth Trust, 1960, p. 14.
7. Ellison, *Men Spake from God,* p. 117.
8. According to Joyce Baldwin's dating (*Tyndale Commentary,* p. 29).
9. As above, p. 20.
10. As above.
11. G. R. Beasley-Murray, *New Bible Commentary,* IVP 1970, p. 1308.

Chapter 2
1. Alan Cole, *Haggai,* Anzea Books, 1976, p. 13.
2. Herbert Wolf, *Haggai and Malachi,* Moody Press, Chicago, 1976, p. 14.
3. See Theo Laetsch, *The Minor Prophets,* Concordia, U.S.A., 1956, p. 383.
4. 549 as at 13 May 1987, according to *The Independent* of that date.

Chapter 3
1.   John Calvin, *The Minor Prophets,* Associated Publisher and
     Authors Inc., Grand Rapids, U.S.A., p. 798.
2.   Baldwin, *Tyndale Commentary,* p. 40.
3.   Cole, Haggai, p. 15.

Chapter 4
1.   Calvin, *Minor Prophets,* p. 804.
2.   Wolf, *Haggai and Malachi,* p. 24.
3.   Baldwin, *Tyndale Commentary,* p. 42.
4.   Calvin, *Minor Prophets,* p. 805.
5.   Wolf, *Haggai and Malachi,* p. 25.

Chapter 5
1.   C. Wordsworth, *Notes in the Holy Bible,* Rivingtons, 1870, p.
     117.
2.   Moore, *Haggai and Malachi,* p. 73.
3.   Laetsch, *Minor Prophets,* p. 393.
4.   Moore, *Haggai and Malachi,* p. 76.
5.   Laetsch, *Minor Prophets,* p. 397.
6.   I am indebted to T. Laetsch for ideas in this section.

Chapter 6
1.   Moore, *Haggai and Malachi,* p. 83.
2.   Baldwin, *Tyndale Commentary,* p. 51.
3.   Wolf, *Haggai and Malachi,* p. 46.
4.   Laetsch, *Minor Prophets,* p. 400.

Chapter 7
1.   Calvin, *Minor Prophets,* p. 826.
2.   Cole, Haggai, p. 37.
3.   Laetsch, *Minor Prophets,* p. 402.
4.   Wolf, *Haggai and Malachi,* p. 53.
5.   Stuart Olyott in a tape recording of a Bible study on Haggai
     (Carey Recordings No. SOB 1818a).
6.   Baldwin, *Tyndale Commentary,* p. 55.
7.   Wolf, *Haggai and Malachi,* p. 53.
8.   Calvin, *Minor Prophets,* p. 825.
9.   David Jackman, *Understanding the Church,* Kingsway
     Publications, 1987, p. 72.

Chapter 8
1.   Both quotations are taken from John Blanchard, *Gathered
     Gold,* Evangelical Press, 1984, pp. 226, 227.

Chapter 9
1. J. Vernon MacGee in *Through the Bible* broadcast on Trans World Radio, Monto Carlo, on 30 December 1987.
2. David Baron, *The Visions and Prophecies of Zechariah,* London, 1918, p. 9.
3. *The NIV Study Bible,* Hodder and Stoughton, 1987, pp. 1377-8.

Chapter 11
1. G. Coleman Luck, *Zechariah,* Moody Press, Chicago, 1957, p. 19.
2. Laetsch, *Minor Prophets,* p. 414.

Chapter 12
1. Jamieson, Fausset and Brown, *Commentary,* p. 664.
2. Laetsch, *Minor Prophets,* p. 418.
3. See chapter 2, p. 25 for a discussion on Zerubbabel and Sheshbazzar.
4. Coleman Luck, *Zechariah,* p. 31.
5. G. C. Leupold, *Exposition of Zechariah,* Baker Book House, Grand Rapids, U.S.A., 1971, p. 59.
6. Moore, *Zechariah,* Banner of Truth Trust, 1958, p. 60.

Chapter 13
1. Moore, *Zechariah,* p. 63.
2. Leupold, *Zechariah,* p. 67.
3. *NIV Study Bible,* p. 1381.
4. Laetsch, *Minor Prophets,* p. 421.
5. Leupold, *Zechariah,* p. 78.

Chapter 14
1. Calvin, *Minor Prophets,* p. 870.
2. Leupold, *Zechariah,* p. 85.

Chapter 15
1. See chapter 3, pp. 37-8.
2. Coleman Luck, *Zechariah,* p. 57.

Chapter 16
1. Stuart Briscoe, *Taking God Seriously,* Word Publishing, 1986, p. 169.
2. Moore, *Zechariah,* p. 87.
3. Baldwin, *Tyndale Commentary,* p. 131.
4. Isaac Watts, 'I'm not ashamed to own my Lord.'

5. Leupold, *Zechariah,* pp. 117-8.
6. See pp. 127-8.
7. Moore, *Zechariah,* p. 97.
8. C. John Miller, *Outgrowing the Ingrown Church,* Zondervan, Grand Rapids, 1986, pp. 61-2.

Chapter 17
1. Leupold, *Zechariah,* p. 130.
2. Quoted in Leupold, *Zechariah,* p. 137.
3. Jamieson, Fausset and Brown, p. 682.
4. Hawker, *Minor Prophets,* p. 512.
5. For a fuller treatment of this subject, see Erroll Hulse, *The Restoration of Israel,* Henry E. Walter, Worthing, 1968.
6. Edmund P. Clowney on 'Kingdom Evangelism' in *The Pastor-Evangelist,* ed. Roger S. Greenway, Presbyterian and Reformed Pub. Co., New Jersey, 1987, p. 25.
7. As above, p. 27.

Chapter 18
1. Quoted in Laetsch, *Minor Prophets,* p. 451.
2. Moore, *Zechariah,* p. 143.
3. Laetsch, *Minor Prophets,* p. 457.

Chapter 19
1. Baldwin, *Tyndale Commentary,* p. 170.
2. W. Hendriksen, *Galatians and Ephesians,* Banner of Truth Trust, p. 143.
3. Leupold, *Zechariah,* p. 201.
4. Calvin, *Minor Prophets,* p. 956.

Chapter 20
1. James Ayre, *In That Day, An Exposition of the Final Destiny of Israel according to Zechariah,* Myrtle Vale, Cheadle, 1986, p. 205.
2. Moore, *Zechariah,* p. 171.
3. Laetsch, *Minor Prophets,* p. 471.
4. Leupold, *Zechariah,* p. 209.
5. Baldwin, *Tyndale Commentary,* p. 181.
6. Ayre, *In That Day,* p. 217.

Chapter 21
1. *NIV Study Bible,* p. 1003.
2. Laetsch, *Minor Prophets,* p. 479.
3. As above, p. 481.

4. Leupold, *Zechariah*, p. 236.
5. Laetsch, *Minor Prophets*, p. 485.
6. C. H. Spurgeon, *The Metropolitan Tabernacle Pulpit*, Passmore and Alabaster, 1897, vol. 43, p. 146.

Chapter 22
1. R. E. Higginson, in *The New Bible Commentary Revised*, ed. D. Guthrie *et. al.* 1970, IVP, p. 811.
2. Coleman Luck, *Zechariah*, p. 115.

Chapter 23
1. A. C. Ainger in the hymn which begins, 'God is working his purpose out'.
2. Ayre, *In That Day*, p. 283.
3. As above, p. 287.
4. Baldwin, *Tyndale Commentary*, p. 207.
5. Leslie Allen, *Hosea-Malachi*, Scripture Union, 1987, p. 119.

EXODUS
Travelling Homeward
Exodus Simply Explained
Michael Bentley

Michael Bentley provides a clear,
organized exposition of Scripture. His
down-to-earth style helps students of
Scripture, whether preachers or their
congregations, to grasp the meaning of the text without
unnecessary difficulty.

Large paperback, 352 pages, 0 85234 429 5
'...informative, incisive and superb in application...'
John Tindall

1 SAMUEL
Dawn of a Kingdom
The message of 1 Samuel
Gordon J. Keddie

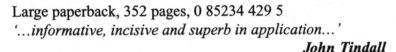

The absolute sovereignty of God and the
triumph of his righteousness are the
principal themes of 1 Samuel. In tracing
the development of Israel from the
anarchy of the period of Judges — from
Samuel the prophet and kingmaker
through Saul, the people's choice, to David, God's chosen
king — the hand of God is seen at work.

Large paperback, 272 pages, 0 85234 248 9
A useful commentary in this fine series.

ECCLESIASTES and SONG of SOLOMON
A Life worth Living and a Lord worth Loving
An exposition of Ecclesiastes and Song of Solomon

Here is a heart-warming and practical explanation of these two often-neglected Old Testament books.

Large paperback, 121 pages
0 85234 173 3

'*Immensely attractive, the book does not disappoint in any way*'

Evangelical Times

LAMENTATIONS
Great is your Faithfulness
Lamentations simply explained
Richard Brooks

Richard Brooks deals with territory which is unfamiliar to most Christians and yet speaks of the abiding themes of the spiritual glory of the church and the tragedy when this is lost. It is a helpful book.

Large paperback, 160 pages
0 85234 257 8

'*This book will stimulate holy living and prove useful as an introduction for those who have never grappled with Lamentations.*'

Banner of Truth

DANIEL
Dare to Stand Alone
Read and enjoy the book of Daniel
Stuart Olyott

A commentary that draws out the
immense amount of practical help to be
found in Daniel's prophecy.

Large paperback, 168 pages
0 85234 163 6

'Makes compulsive reading'

Grace Magazine

JONAH
Preacher on the Run
The message of Jonah
Gordon J. Keddie

A fresh look at the book of Jonah which
puts the dramatic Bible story into
perspective within Israel's history and
teaches that the story is practical and
relevant for today.

Large paperback, 134 pages, 0 85234 230 6

*'...commended for its solid and practical exposition ... this
volume should be widely read.'*

Moorlands College

MALACHI
Losing Touch with the Living God
The message of Malachi
John Benton

John Benton shows how Malachi's book
is a call from lax and hollow religion,
pointing the way back to genuine,
enduring faith in the Lord who does not
change

Large paperback, 140 pages
0 85234 212 8

ROMANS
The Gospel as it Really is
Paul's epistle to the Romans simply explained
Stuart Olyott

The author's clear and easy style leads the
reader to a greater understanding of this
important epistle. It is ideal as an
introduction to the gospel for new
converts who may work through Dr
Olyott's clear and well-illustrated
presentation of God's grace shown in the
work of the Lord Jesus Christ.

Large paperback, 165 pages
0 85234 125 3

'The work exhibits interpretative mastery...'

F. F. Bruce

JOHN'S EPISTLES
Knowing where we Stand
The message of John's epistles
Peter Barnes

In days of spiritual and moral decline we stand in particular need of the message of John's epistles. Right belief, love and obedience are the principal themes explored in this book.

Large paperback, 160 pages, 0 85234 414 7
'...excellent, thorough, stimulating, informed...'
        John Currid, *Reformed Theological Seminary, Jackson*

JUDE
Slandering the Angels
Jude simply explained
John Benton

Christians may be open to accept anything that causes a sensation and attracts a crowd, even if it departs from the biblical gospel. This commentary helps to combat false teaching and encourages responsible Christian living and practical, loving Christianity for those led astray.

Large paperback, 192 pages, 0 85234 424 4
'...illuminating exegesis, a fresh and lucid style, a wonderful sprinkling of appropriate and helpful illustrations...'

                                Banner of Truth

REVELATION
The Lamb is all the glory
The book of Revelation
Richard Brooks

The author comes afresh to the message
of the book of Revelation with a warm
pastoral exposition that feeds the heart as
well as the mind of the reader.

Large paperback, 222 pages
0 85234 229 2

'*Buy it, and use it prayerfully; your Christian life will be
stirred by the glorious display of Christ's person and
victory.*'

Grace Magazine

Welwyn Commentaries on the Old Testament

EXODUS *Travelling Homeward*
Michael Bentley
0 85234 429 5 Large paperback, 352pp.

NUMBERS *According to Promise*
Gordon J. Keddie
0 85234 295 0 Large paperback, 224pp.

JUDGES & RUTH *Even in Darkness*
Gordon J. Keddie
0 85234 201 2 Large paperback, 128pp.

1 SAMUEL *Dawn of a Kingdom*
Gordon J. Keddie
0 85234 248 9 Large paperback, 272pp.

2 SAMUEL *Triumph of the King*
Gordon J. Keddie
0 85234 272 1 Large paperback, 272pp.

1 CHRONICLES *A Family Tree*
Andrew Stewart
0 85234 393 0 Large paperback, 224pp.

EZRA & NEHEMIAH *Doing a Great Work*
Stan K. Evers
0 85234 346 9 Large paperback, 224pp.

JOB *The Storm Breaks*
Derek Thomas
0 85234 336 1 Large paperback, 352pp.

ECCLESIASTES & SONG OF SOLOMON
A Life worth Living and a Lord worth Loving
Stuart Olyott
0 85234 173 3 Large paperback, 128pp.

ISAIAH *God Delivers*
Derek Thomas
0 85234 290 X Large paperback, 416pp.

LAMENTATIONS *Great is your Faithfulness*
Richard Brooks
0 85234 257 8 Large paperback, 160pp.

EZEKIEL *God Strengthens*, Derek Thomas
0 85234 310 8 Large paperback, 320pp.

DANIEL *Dare to Stand Alone*
Stuart Olyott
0 85234 163 5 Large paperback, 176pp.

JOEL *Prophet of the Coming Day of the Lord*
O. Palmer Robertson
0 85234 335 3 Large paperback, 112pp.

AMOS *The Lord is his Name*
Gordon J. Keddie
0 85234 224 1 Large paperback, 112pp.

JONAH *Preacher on the Run*
Gordon J. Keddie
0 85234 231 4 Large paperback, 144pp.

MICAH & NAHUM *Balancing the Books*
Michael Bentley
0 85234 324 8 Large paperback, 128pp.

HAGGAI & ZECHARIAH *Building for God's Glory*
Michael Bentley
0 85234 259 4 Large paperback, 240pp.

MALACHI *Losing Touch with the Living God*
John Benton
0 85234 212 8 Large paperback, 140pp.

Welwyn Commentaries on the New Testament

LUKE *Saving a Fallen World*
Michael Bentley
0 85234 300 0 Large paperback, 336pp.

ACTS OF THE APOSTLES *You are my Witnesses*
Gordon J. Keddie
0 85234 307 8 Large paperback, 336pp.

ROMANS *The Gospel as it Really is*
Stuart Olyott
0 85234 125 3 Large paperback, 176pp.

1 CORINTHIANS
Strengthening Christ's Church
Roger Ellsworth
0 85234 333 7 Large paperback, 272pp.

GALATIANS *Free in Christ*
Edgar H. Andrews
0 85234 353 1 Large paperback, 320pp.

EPHESIANS *Alive in Christ*
Stuart Olyott
0 85234 315 9 Large paperback, 144pp.

PHILIPPIANS *Shining in the Darkness*
Michael Bentley
0 85234 403 1 Large paperback, 192pp.

1 & 2 THESSALONIANS *Patience of Hope*
J. Philip Arthur
0 85234 385 X Large paperback, 160pp.

1 & 2 TIMOTHY *Passing on the Truth*
Michael Bentley
0 85234 389 2 Large paperback, 320pp.

TITUS *Straightening out the Self-centred Church,*
John Benton
0 85234 384 1 Large paperback 192pp.

JAMES *The Practical Christian,*
Gordon J. Keddie
0 85234 261 6 Large paperback, 240pp.

JOHN'S EPISTLES *Knowing where we Stand,*
Peter Barnes
0 85234 414 7 Large paperback,   160pp.

1 & 2 PETER *Living for Christ in a Pagan World*
Michael Bentley
0 85234 279 9 Large paperback,   256pp.

JUDE *Slandering the Angels*
John Benton
0 85234 424 4 Large paperback, 192pp.

REVELATION *The Lamb is all the Glory*
Richard Brooks
0 85234 229 2 Large paperback, 224pp.